SKILLS & VALUES:
DISCOVERY PRACTICE

SKILLS & VALUES; DISCOVERY PRACTICE

Second Edition

David I. C. Thomson
LP Professor
University of Denver, Sturm College of Law

ISBN: 978–1–6328–1222–3 (softbound)
ebook ISBN: 978-1-6328-1223-0

Library of Congress Cataloging-in-Publication Data

Thomson, David I. C., author.
Skills & values. Discovery practice / David I.C. Thomson, LP Professor, University of Denver, Sturm College of Law. -- Second Edition.
pages cm
ISBN 978-1-63281-222-3 (softbound)
1. Discovery (Law)--United States--Problems, exercises, etc. I. Title. II. Title: Discovery practic. III. Title: Skills and values.
KF8900.T48 2014
347.73'72--dc23   2014041160

This publication is designed to provide authoritative information in regard to the subject matter covered. It is sold with the understanding that the publisher is not engaged in rendering legal, accounting, or other professional services. If legal advice or other expert assistance is required, the services of a competent professional should be sought.

NOTE TO USERS

To ensure that you are using the latest materials available in this area, please be sure to periodically check the LexisNexis Law School web site for downloadable updates and supplements at www.lexisnexis.com/lawschool.

Editorial Offices
630 Central Ave., New Providence, NJ 07974 (908) 464-6800
201 Mission St., San Francisco, CA 94105-1831 (415) 908-3200
www.lexisnexis.com

MATTHEW♦BENDER

To Kathy

With gratitude

for all your love and support

Forward to the Second Edition

As more and more law schools look for ways to increase their experiential learning opportunities, expanding clinics and externships can only go so far. What is also needed is an expansion of courses based on a simulation model that are designed to prepare students for those clinical and externship opportunities, and also for practice after graduation. Further, while the Carnegie report not only articulated the "three apprenticeships" of legal education — doctrine, skills, and professional identity formation — it also argued in favor of *integrating* the apprenticeships as much as possible in law school courses. One of the strengths of simulation courses is that they are well suited to achieve such integration, since they involve teaching legal doctrine through skills training, and they do so in a way that places students in the role of attorneys, which also allows many opportunities for professional formation. Further, a *whole-course* simulation can be terrifically effective in achieving this goal by teaching the doctrine of a particular subject placed fully in the most common practice context, allowing students to be "in role" for the entire semester.

The first edition of this hybrid textbook was well received by numerous adopting professors looking for a book that would support teaching the material in exactly this sort of simulation-based experiential format. They took to its extraordinary flexibility, since only the basic principles are printed here in this book, and the fully populated companion online Web Course that is used with the book allowed for teachers to work with the materials in a way that fit their particular learning goals, and to easily add or subtract as needed. Some of those professors have used this text in a traditional pre-trial course, and others have used it in courses focused only on the discovery rules. It works either way. It has even been used in a law firm as part of an in-house training course for new members of the firm's litigation department.

The second edition of *Skills & Values: Discovery Practice* improves on the original in a number of ways. Adjustments were made to the time estimates for the assignments at the end of each chapter. These adjustments were based on feedback from students who actually completed the assignments over five semesters of my teaching the course, using the book and online site. Also, the problem set materials have been updated with a few minor errors corrected, but they now feature a flexible dating scheme so the problem will not go out of date and the professor may easily make adjustments to the problem each year that they use it.

I welcome your feedback on the textbook — whether you are an adopting professor or a student. I have written more extensively about my own experience using this book on the *Law School 2.0* blog. You will find those posts here — http://bit.ly/lawtexts.

David Thomson
University of Denver
October 2, 2014

Introduction

In law school, all first year students take Civil Procedure — the study of the litigation process under the Federal Rules of Civil Procedure (FRCP). Unfortunately, few courses — and even the assigned casebooks — provide much instruction on the twelve FRCP that relate to and manage the process of discovery: the period in a litigation when parties exchange information in preparation for settlement or trial. This is quite peculiar because in the practice of law most of the working time of a litigator is spent in the discovery phase, for two reasons. First, the discovery phase in litigation is much longer than are most trials. But more significantly, fewer than 2 percent of civil cases filed in Federal Court today even go to trial. Law schools usually have plenty of trial practice classes, and no doubt they teach useful and important skills. But students who want to practice civil litigation should take a course in discovery law. If during their law school career they did not take such a course — perhaps because their school did not offer one — and they join a litigation firm (or litigation department of a larger firm) they will quickly find themselves at a deficit. That is because the subject of this book, discovery, is the part of civil procedure they will find themselves using the most often — and yet the one they are often the least prepared to practice.

This book is intended to remedy this situation, either by supporting the teaching of such a course in law school, or as a supplement for newly-minted attorneys who did not have the benefit of such a course. It is meant to serve as an introduction to the practical application of the discovery rules by introducing each topic briefly, and providing a context and structure for exercises and self-study. It can be used by a professor teaching a full pre-trial course, or one focused just on discovery law. It can be used alone or in conjunction with another pre-trial text. It can be used with the problem set provided in the appendix (and online), or with a professor's own problem set. Finally, it can easily be used in a mentorship program in a civil litigation law firm.

Each chapter offers an introduction to the key aspects of discovery and then offers exercises that focus on the governing Federal Rule of Civil Procedure (FRCP). The chapters are organized in the order that the discovery rules are most commonly used. In practice, of course, they are often used in a different order than they are presented here — and they sometimes overlap — so these chapters could easily be addressed in a different order as well. The exercises at the end of each chapter ask the student to put the governing rules into action by actually drafting the discovery documents described in the preceding chapter.

This book is focused on the *Federal* Rules of Civil Procedure, and does not address the occasional variations that exist in various State-based discovery rules. This is primarily for the sake of expediency – there is more variation in state rules than is possible to effectively cover here, and for the most part, the discovery rules in most states either mirror the FRCP or operate much the same way.

Because the discovery process involves an *exchange* of information, the exercises in this book are most instructive when they are done in conjunction with an assigned opposing counsel — another student or colleague — so that each student can prepare the assigned discovery document and "serve" it on his or her opposing counsel. That way they also receive a discovery document to which they need to prepare an answer. This process

Introduction

continues through the course. It works best when each student is provided with only his or her side's portion of the available problem information which allows the student to learn both how to write the requesting document and respond to one that requests information as well. This approach creates a simulated litigation environment where student attorneys on each side spend the semester actually using the discovery documents they are learning about to obtain the information they need to prepare a case for trial or settlement.

Each chapter includes some self-study guidance, and online, offers a self-assessment exercise. These can be used by the student alone or in conjunction with a teacher or mentor who can provide additional feedback on some or all of the exercises. These aspects of the book are designed to help in building skills as well as judgment: the federal rules set the parameters of what *can* be done, but the goal of this book is for students to begin to develop good judgment about what *should* be done under a given set of circumstances. As a result, there are no perfect answers to the questions presented in this book. They are, instead, designed to prepare the student for the practice of civil litigation where a mix of rule comprehension, strategy, judgment, and ethical balancing all come into play.

Each chapter also includes electronic materials, which the student may access by visiting the **LexisNexis Web Course** site, and obtaining access to the **Web Course** that goes with the book. (Lexis Publishing representatives can help with this process). These materials include problem sets to work with, documentary information, video clips, example discovery documents, checklists, and links to the complete rules, important case law, and other supporting information.

Organization of the Book

Each chapter contains:

An introduction that puts the chapter within the context of the actual day-to-day practice of law.

The relevant section of the Federal Rules of Civil Procedure.

An assignment in which the student can practice the skills learned in the chapter.

Example documents from which to begin to prepare the assignment (online).

A self-assessment section the student can use after he or she has completed the assignment.

Acknowledgments

As with all such efforts, this book would not exist without the help and support of many people other than the listed author, and I would like to express my gratitude to them. First I must thank the many students at the University of Denver's Sturm College of Law who have made their way through the course upon which this book is based. I have taught a course called Discovery Practicum at the law school on and off for 22 years. In those years, I have taught the course over a dozen times times with approximately 20 students in each administration of the course. I cannot thank 300 students individually, but I can thank them collectively. And I must, because without their eagerness to learn this material and willingness to try a different way of learning, I might have retreated to a more conventional approach. Indeed, their enthusiasm for this approach to law teaching has also taught me much, and encouraged me in these efforts. But more importantly, I suspect that I have learned as much from them about Discovery law as I think they have learned from me.

While virtually all scholarly production requires the assistance of students, this book is particularly indebted to the work of Eileen Joy (Class of 2010), who worked tirelessly on many parts of it. Having been a student of mine in Lawyering Process in her first year, she took the Discovery class in her second year, and became my primary research assistant in her third year. Having taken the class on which this book is based, she was able to create initial drafts of many of the chapters based on what she learned there. Because she was both a terrific student and had the experience of taking the class, she has also helped to ensure that the book has the student focus and orientation to practice that the course has always had.

In addition to Eileen, I am indebted to Ian London (Class of 2011) who read drafts of many of the chapters and improved them with his comments. I am also grateful to Kendra Beckwith (Class of 2008) who developed parts of the problem set that is provided in the Appendix and online. Also many thanks to Beth Tomerlin (Class of 2007) who took the class, and then started her career in civil litigation. In reviewing a draft of the book she was able to provide insights from current practice that were very helpful. Also, thanks to Kelley Haun and Edgar Barraza, who both took the course in 2014, and assisted me with the second edition. My editors at Lexis, Christine Frost, Keith Moore, and Leslie Levin, helped to improve this book in myriad ways as well. Also, I am extremely grateful to my father, David S. Thomson, for offering many thoughtful and precise editing suggestions on an earlier version of this manuscript. In addition, my dearly departed (and much missed) colleague Professor Ann Scales added terrific suggestions in her review of the manuscript, and brought her characteristic combination of comprehensive knowledge and rapier wit to the effort.

I am particularly indebted to Dean Marty Katz and Associate Dean for Scholarship Alan Chen for supporting this work with a summer stipend in the summers of 2009 and 2010. I remain grateful for the mentoring over the years provided by former Associate Dean Fred Cheever, who continues to be supportive of my work in this area.

Finally, I am deeply grateful for the love and support of my wife Kathy and our two children Angelina and Sarah-Jane. I could not do this work without their help and understanding.

Table of Contents

Table of Contents

Chapter 1

PLANNING FOR DISCOVERY

OVERVIEW

One of the most important steps in a new or impending litigation is to prepare a plan. Most legal cases begin with a client interview, which focuses on the client's situation, needs, and desired outcome. After a period typically spent in factual investigation and legal research, the attorney will counsel the client on the best available options to achieve the client's goals. If litigation is determined to be the best option, then it is time to develop a plan for it. In this phase, the attorney has an obligation to explain to the client the most likely course of the litigation, and to review its costs and benefits. This is not possible unless a litigation plan has already been prepared.

A litigation plan starts with identifying potential claims and defenses, which naturally requires some legal research. It is important at this stage to also conduct some factual investigation, such as reviewing any available documents and conducting third party witness interviews (if available). These steps lead to the preparation of a complaint (or answer if a complaint has been filed against the client). Once the complaint and answer have been filed, it is time to plan the discovery phase of the litigation.

As will be clear in the next chapter, the first stage of discovery is the preparation of initial disclosures, so the process of preparing what must be disclosed at this stage of the litigation comes first. After that, the focus is on what information is not known and which must be obtained in discovery for the case to be ready for trial (or settlement negotiations). Further, the plan should be as specific as possible about which discovery instrument will be used to obtain which information. Thus, the plan should categorize the information needed by the best tool to obtain that information: Interrogatories (Chapter 3), Document Requests (Chapter 5), Expert Witnesses (Chapter 9), Depositions (Chapter 10), and Requests to Admit (Chapter 11). Today, many clients ask their attorneys to estimate the cost of the discovery phase of litigation, so after the plan is prepared a spreadsheet with estimates of hours to be worked by specific attorneys and paralegals (including their respective billing rates) will be required.

Because cases in the discovery phase rarely go smoothly, it would be wise for the plan to include time spent filing (or responding to) Motions to Compel (Chapter 8) and handling any discovery disputes short of actually filing a motion. Because most litigations end in settlement, it should also set aside time for the negotiating and drafting of a settlement agreement.

Making predictions about how the case will progress through the discovery phase is an inherently inexact process, but with experience and practice, this can be done with some level of confidence. It is wise for an attorney to counsel his or her client on the unpredictable nature of discovery. In addition, the relative success or failure of each phase of the discovery process — as well as the nature of what is discovered — will determine the most appropriate next step in the litigation (which may be different from the original plan). Therefore, the litigation plan is a living document, and should be updated throughout the litigation, and reviewed with the client periodically.

It is also at this early stage that setting up a process for collecting and using the information obtained in discovery is important. While many offices still use paper files, law offices increasingly rely on electronic tools to keep track of the myriad details in a litigation. One of the best of these, CaseMap, is made available by Lexis for free to all law professors and their students. It is recommended that the student using this text use CaseMap to categorize and track the information they obtain using the discovery documents during the course. CaseMap may be obtained through a link located at http://www.lexisnexis.com/lawschool or at http://www.casesoft.com.

EXERCISE:

Prepare a litigation plan, including a chart listing information you already know that you will need to obtain in discovery, based on the simulated problem information you have been provided. Use that chart to prepare a spreadsheet detailing estimated costs for the discovery phase of the litigation. Also, prepare a brief memo to the file explaining the decisions you made and strategy you implemented in preparing your litigation plan.

ESTIMATED TIME FOR COMPLETING THIS EXERCISE: Three hours.

LEVEL OF DIFFICULTY: Moderate

AS YOU PREPARE THIS ASSIGNMENT, CONSIDER THE FOLLOWING:

Have you conducted initial legal research on the nature of the matter in dispute?

Have you identified the claims and defenses in your litigation?

Have you prepared a chart of information needed in discovery?

Does the plan categorize needed information by the discovery mechanism you will use to obtain that information?

Have you prepared a spreadsheet, including hourly rates of attorneys and paralegals who will work on the litigation, so as to provide a reasonable estimate of the cost of discovery to your client?

Have you included some estimate of the cost of discovery disputes that might arise?

Have you created the initial CaseMap file for the litigation, containing the basic information you have learned about your case to this point?

ONLINE:

In the **LexisNexis Web Course**, you will find an example chart of Information needed in Discovery, as well as an example spreadsheet for developing cost estimates. There is also an example CaseMap file, and links to download a trial copy of CaseMap to your computer.

Chapter 2

INITIAL DISCLOSURES

OVERVIEW

FRCP 26(a)(1) includes three separate types of required disclosures: initial disclosures, expert disclosures, and pre-trial disclosures. This chapter addresses initial disclosures. (Expert disclosures, Rule 26(a)(B) are discussed in Chapter 9 and pre-trial disclosures, Rule 26(a)(1)(C), are addressed in Chapter 13). Rule 26(a)(1) details what sorts of discoverable information must be disclosed in the initial disclosures and establishes when and how that information must be provided to the opposing party. Initial disclosures will typically be the first discovery step any attorney will take in the pre-trial stage. Unlike all other forms of discovery, attorneys do not have to request initial disclosures, since each has an affirmative obligation to prepare and serve them on the other side. And they must do so promptly: Rule 26(a)(1) requires each attorney to provide the other with initial disclosures "at or within 14 days after the parties' Rule 26(f) conference."[1]

What Do Initial Disclosures Include?

Initial disclosures must include names and contact information of people who may have discoverable information; identification of documents, files, or materials that the party may use in their defense; computation of damages; and insurance agreements, which may be used in the case to cover all or part of a damage award.[2]

Rule 26

    (a) Required Disclosures.

        (1) Initial Disclosure.

            (A) In General. Except as exempted by Rule 26(a)(1)(B) or as otherwise stipulated or ordered by the court, a party must, without awaiting a discovery request, provide to the other parties:

                (i) the name and, if known, the address and telephone number of each individual likely to have discoverable information — along with the subjects of that information — that the disclosing party may use to support its claims or defenses, unless the use would be solely for impeachment;

---

[1] That 14-day time limit is subject to adjustment, if the parties stipulate to a different timeframe under Rule 29 or if the court orders otherwise. FRCP 26(a)(1)(C).

[2] Fed. R. Civ. P. 26(a)(1)(A)-(D).

     (ii) a copy — or a description by category and location — of all documents, electronically stored information, and tangible things that the disclosing party has in its possession, custody, or control and may use to support its claims or defenses, unless the use would be solely for impeachment;

     (iii) a computation of each category of damages claimed by the disclosing party — who must also make available for inspection and copying as under Rule 34 the documents or other evidentiary material, unless privileged or protected from disclosure, on which each computation is based, including materials bearing on the nature and extent of injuries suffered; and

     (iv) for inspection and copying as under Rule 34, any insurance agreement under which an insurance business may be liable to satisfy all or part of a possible judgment in the action or to indemnify or reimburse for payments made to satisfy the judgment.

Initial disclosures play an important role in discovery because they allow each party to determine what route to take at the beginning of the litigation. Your client will have already provided you with names of key people, contact information for them, and perhaps specific damages information. As long as that information is not otherwise privileged, if it fits within a 26(a)(1)(A) category, and it supports your claims or defenses, you must disclose it in your initial disclosures. On the other hand, if you have documents that may be subject to a privilege — such as the attorney-client privilege — then you do not have to disclose them. You should, however, prepare a privilege log that identifies the documents on which you are asserting a privilege, and submit that document with your initial disclosures.

There are many advantages to the initial disclosures requirement. In effect, initial disclosures provide you with a compass at the outset of discovery. And in so doing they set up the first set of interrogatories, which are addressed in the next chapter. Because interrogatories are limited to twenty-five (unless otherwise stipulated or ordered) you can use them to expand on information you learn from the initial disclosures.

When must Initial Disclosures Be Provided?

As noted above, the rule states that initial disclosures must be provided, "at or within 14 days after the parties' Rule 26(f) conference." However, the parties may rely on Rule 29 if they mutually agree that the 14-day timeline is insufficient. Rule 29 stipulations apply to almost all discovery requests. Litigation is a contentious process, but generally being reasonable with your opposing counsel, especially with stipulation requests for reasonable time extensions, may benefit you in both the short term and the long.

For example, opposing counsel may ask you to stipulate to a 14-day extension for initial disclosures because he or she is in the middle of a trial, which will not end until two days before the 14-day post-conference deadline. There are three fundamental questions you must ask yourself before responding to such a request: (1) do you have any discovery plans that are absolutely dependent on receiving those initial disclosures by the Rule's required deadline or is a 14-day extension inconsequential; (2) in the short term, how thorough do you expect opposing counsel's initial disclosures to be if you say no (after all, he can supplement disclosures at a later date); and (3) in the long term, what do you know about opposing counsel — is he reasonable and would he be likely to stipulate to one of your discovery extension requests if the situation arises in the future?

Although initial disclosures must be provided within 14 days following the 26(f) conference, additional information that falls under an initial disclosure category may come to light in the ensuing weeks or months. When that occurs, Rule 26(e) requires the parties to supplement their initial disclosures "in a timely manner." The language of that rule follows:

(e) **Supplementing Disclosures and Responses.**

(1) In General. A party who has made a disclosure under Rule 26(a) — or who has responded to an interrogatory, request for production, or request for admission — must supplement or correct its disclosure or response:

(A) in a timely manner if the party learns that in some material respect the disclosure or response is incomplete or incorrect, and if the additional or corrective information has not otherwise been made known to the other parties during the discovery process or in writing;

(B) as ordered by the court.

This aspect of the rule is an example of an ethical dilemma that can arise during discovery. What exactly is "a timely manner?" Is it the next day, or a week after you learn of the new information? Judgment, as always, is important. If the new information is crucial to the case, revealing as soon as is practicable would be within the spirit and intent of the rules. If the time remaining before trial is short, the speed with which it would be disclosed should increase.

Preparing to Draft Initial Disclosures

What to Ethically Disclose?

The biggest problem that initial disclosures pose is determining how much information you must provide and when you have to provide it. The language in the rules often leaves a lot of room for interpretation. Rule 26(a)(1)(A)-(D) appears to require only basic information and in some instances minimal descriptive information. Therefore, while "a party must, without awaiting a discovery request, provide" the initial disclosures to the opposing party, the effect of this mandate is diminished because (A)-(D) do not require great detail in those disclosures. Essentially, the spirit of 26(a)(1)(A) is to start out by playing fair. Further, the due date for supplemental disclosures is vague. What is "a timely manner?" There is a lot of gray area in the discovery process and attorneys frequently encounter the countervailing issues of effective and diligent advocacy for their client and the fundamental principle of good faith and fair play when dealing with opposing counsel and the courts.[3]

When such gray areas and ethical considerations arise, there are usually three places to begin making a decision about what to do: the relevant rule of civil procedure, the discovery request you are replying to, and the ethics rules. If the discovery and ethical rules still have not provided the guidance you need, look at the comments to the rules. In addition to the sources noted above, local case law may provide guidance. If it is a timeliness issue and you find yourself resorting to case law, you may have already answered your question – you are probably pushing the boundaries.

Rule 26(a)(1) requires you to scrutinize the language of the rule and ask yourself, "what exactly must I disclose?" For example, 26(a)(1)(A) requires "the name and, if known, the address and telephone number of each individual likely to have discoverable information that the disclosing party may use to support its claims or defenses, unless solely for impeachment, identifying the subjects of the information." Careful reading indicates that you must provide a name. However, contact information need only be provided "if known." To what ends of the earth must you go to "know" this contact information? Rule 26(a)(1)(E) is a good place to start for clarification:

(E) **Basis for Initial Disclosure; Unacceptable Excuses.**

A party must make its initial disclosures based on the information then *reasonably available to it.* A party is *not excused* from making its disclosures *because it has not fully investigated the case* or because it challenges the sufficiency of another party's disclosures or because another party has not made its disclosures. *(emphasis added)*

The terms "if known" and "reasonably available" do not provide a hard and fast rule, but "reasonably available" appears to mean that some effort must be made. Model Rule of Professional Conduct 3.4 coincides with this unclear standard. It states that an attorney, "shall not: . . . (d) in pre-trial, make a frivolous discovery request or fail to make reasonably diligent effort to comply with a legally proper discovery request by an opposing party."[4] The lesson to take away from this is that most discovery rules allow the attorney to effectively advocate for his or her client, but ethics rules require a standard of reasonable professionalism and fairness toward the opposing party. However, it is up to each attorney to navigate the rules and determine how far the reasonableness standard applies to each disclosure.

It is important to keep in mind that you also owe a duty to the court. If your actions during discovery are not reasonable, the other party may seek assistance of the court to issue a Rule 37 motion to compel. The initial disclosures stage of discovery is just the beginning of your interactions with the court. A motion to compel ordered against you is not an ideal way to begin a litigation; you do not want to lose credibility with

---

[3] Model Rules of Prof'l Conduct R. 1.3, 1.6, and 3.4 (2009).

[4] Model Rules of Prof'l Conduct R. 3.4.

the judge at any point, and certainly not this early in the process.[5]

Drafting

After you have gathered the relevant information under Rule 26(a)(1)(A), begin drafting the initial disclosures. Below the caption and introduction section, the easiest way to lay out initial disclosures may be under section headings. For example, "Persons Who May Have Discoverable Information" or "Computation of Damages." While the thought may occur to you that this will make it too easy for opposing counsel to use your disclosures, consider this: how easy will it be for you to review and make sufficient use of your disclosures if they are disjointed and unorganized? A good example of disclosures, and their format, is provided in the online portion of this book.

Under each heading, provide your information. Once you have drafted the document, typically in numerical fashion, go back and edit. Ask yourself, "have I only provided what I must?" For example, you must indicate the subject matter that an identified person may testify about. How much must you disclose? Again, reflect upon the ethics rules. You must provide enough information that is reasonable to fairly inform the other party of the topic, but by no means do you have to provide a dissertation on all of the details the witness may possess. Indeed at this stage in the litigation you may not even know.

Although electronically stored information ("ESI") is addressed in more detail in Chapter 6, you should be considering — even this early in the litigation — how you will handle any ESI that your client might possess. If there is such electronic information that comes under the requirements for initial disclosures, you would need to include it as part of your disclosure, whether printed out or in some magnetic form (CD or electronic file sent via e-mail). You should also keep in mind that sometimes clients need considerable assistance from you in gathering such information.

Concerning a damages calculation, you may not yet have those details, or they may only be partially known this early in the litigation. Under such circumstances, it is usually acceptable to include a simple statement such as, "all economic and non-economic damages being sought in this litigation in an amount to be determined at trial along with pre- and post-judgment interest permitted by law."

After the pleading has been drafted, scrutinized, and edited, you must sign it pursuant to Rule 26(g). Not only does this indicate to the other party that it is your official pleading, but it means that the information contained therein adheres to the requirements of Rule 26(a)(1)(E): that all the information was provided in good faith, and is what was reasonably available at the time of the submission.

---

[5] Model Rules of Prof'l Conduct R. 3.3.

EXERCISE:

Prepare initial disclosures in your case with the information you have been provided. Also, prepare a brief memo to the file explaining the decisions you made and strategy you implemented in preparing this discovery document.

ESTIMATED TIME FOR COMPLETING THIS EXERCISE: One to two hours.

LEVEL OF DIFFICULTY: Moderate

AS YOU PREPARE THIS ASSIGNMENT, CONSIDER THE FOLLOWING:

Have you provided the names of people with discoverable information?

Have you provided copies (or description of them and their locations) to all documents that support your claims and defenses?

Have you reviewed all documents, and prepared a privilege log for any documents that are privileged?

Have you provided information about any damages that you have alleged in your complaint or counterclaim?

Have you reviewed, proofread, and signed your document?

Have you prepared a certificate of service for the document?

ONLINE:

In the **LexisNexis Web Course**, you will find an example set of Initial Disclosures with explanatory information.

Chapter 3

INTERROGATORIES

OVERVIEW

A complaint has been filed and served, an answer has also been filed, and initial disclosures have been provided. What should you do next? Of course, by the time you ask that question, you should have a preliminary discovery plan in place, with a rough idea of what information you need at this point in the litigation. Of the common discovery tools — interrogatories, depositions, expert witnesses, and document or electronic discovery requests, what should you use first? Frequently, interrogatories are one of the first discovery tools used because they are inexpensive and if properly used, can help narrow and guide future discovery requests. On the other hand, for strategic purposes it may be wise to save some interrogatories for later use.

What Are Interrogatories?

Interrogatories are written questions served on the other party pursuant to FRCP 33. Interrogatories may inquire into anything that is relevant to the claims or defenses of the case falling within the scope of discovery as defined in FRCP 26(b). Under FRCP 33(a)(1), interrogatories are limited to twenty-five questions. You are not, however, required to send a set of interrogatories that contain all twenty-five at once. If you believe that you would draft certain interrogatories differently based upon the answers you obtain from other interrogatories, hold off on asking those questions and submit them at a later date after you receive and review the initial responses. If you use only fifteen interrogatories up front, you have not forfeited the use of the remaining ten; reserve their use for a later date when they can be more effective.

It may be possible to serve more interrogatories than the twenty-five allowed by Rule 33(a). But pursuant to Rule 26(b)(2)(A), you must have leave of court to do so, upon a showing of good cause. Alternatively, under FRCP 29, both you and opposing counsel may stipulate in writing to more interrogatories. It is wise not to expect the court to grant a motion for additional interrogatories — or opposing counsel to stipulate to additional questions — so plan to use the twenty-five that you are allowed under the rule in a judicious manner.

The Rule in relevant part:

FRCP 33. Interrogatories to Parties

(a) In General.

(1) Number. Unless otherwise stipulated or ordered by the court, a party may serve on any other party no more than 25 written interrogatories, including all discrete subparts. Leave to serve additional interrogatories may be granted to the extent consistent with Rule 26(b)(2).

(2) Scope. An interrogatory may relate to any matter that may be inquired into under Rule 26(b). An interrogatory is not objectionable merely because it asks for an opinion or contention that relates to fact or the application of law to fact, but the court may order that the interrogatory need not be answered until designated discovery is complete, or until a pretrial conference or some other time.

* * *

When to Serve Interrogatories

There is only one timing requirement for service of interrogatories; they may not be served until a Rule 26(f) conference has been held. Following that conference, they may be served without leave of court and without stipulation at any point during discovery. However, they often tend to be most useful when implemented early, before the more cumbersome and expensive types of discovery are initiated.

Because interrogatories are a simple and inexpensive discovery tool, they can be an effective means to guide future discovery requests, yielding more relevant information and preventing undue expense. When used properly, interrogatories can be a prelude to more refined future discovery requests such as Rule 34 Requests for Production of Documents (described in Chapter 5) or Rule 30 Depositions (described in Chapter 10). For example, in a contract dispute, if you believe that certain documents or ESI exist, but do not know who is in possession of them, an interrogatory or two could be a simple and inexpensive way to determine that information and to provide a more refined and expedient basis for future Rule 34 requests. In another example, you might want to know the identity of certain decision makers. By identifying them through interrogatories, you would know whom to depose later on in the litigation. Generally, interrogatories should be used to narrow your legal theory of the case and uncover some basic facts that are relevant to that theory. Although you may find it necessary to hold off on serving all 25 interrogatories upon the other party during the early stages of discovery, serving at least a small set of interrogatories will probably be one of the first discovery tools you utilize.

There are occasions, however, in which interrogatories may be more useful at a later stage of discovery. Court ordered mediation is increasingly imposed on parties in an effort to encourage them to resolve their dispute without having to go to trial. Imagine that you are plaintiff's counsel seeking damages; you have conducted a substantial amount of discovery and you feel confident about your legal position entering mediation. You realize, though, that even if you negotiate a large settlement award for your client, you have no idea how it will be paid. Such a situation may be ideally suited for remaining interrogatories. If you can identify bank accounts, account balances, other assets, and the rate at which income or profits are generated, you will be better armed to enter mediation with the ability to suggest creative means for structuring a settlement and confident that the settlement can be timely paid.

Whether interrogatories are used early or later in the process or split for use in both phases will depend on the case. Ultimately, if carefully drafted, interrogatories can inexpensively and easily provide you with necessary information to move forward and use other discovery tools more effectively.

Structure of Interrogatories

The format of interrogatories is more involved than a simple list of 25 questions. Interrogatory pleadings typically have four parts: (1) the preface; (2) the instructions; (3) the definitions; and (4) the questions themselves. Although the FRCP do not require the first three parts, some state rules may require them, and they are generally used. The preface is brief; it includes but is not limited to who is serving the interrogatories, the FRCP legal basis for them, and information relating to the responses.[6] The other two introductory sections, instructions and definitions, are intended to restrict the opposing party's ability to interpret and answer questions in a manner more beneficial to them than you would prefer. Finally, the questions themselves have different forms: stand alone interrogatories, interrogatories with sub-parts, fact-seeking interrogatories, or contention interrogatories.

Instructions

Although interrogatories are served on the opposing party, that party's attorney will most likely be the first to review them and note objections and provisional answers before the client does. Attorneys should be well versed in and aware of the rules of ethics when responding to any discovery request, along with everything else they do in the practice of law. There is a balance that must be struck between ethically advocating for your client and obstructing discovery.

In advocating for your client, some attorneys strive to avoid answering interrogatories in any way they can to prevent disclosure of information. Between the duty of confidentiality,[7] the work-product doctrine,[8] and the attorney-client privilege,[9] an attorney has many options available to prevent disclosure and to object to interrogatories. Because of this inclination to avoid disclosure, a brief set of instructions should be included in your interrogatories because it can serve as a gentle but professional reminder of the attorney's duty to make a diligent effort in responding to your

---

[6] For example: "Defendant, by and through her counsel, Joe Smith, Esq., requests that ACME, Inc. (ACME) respond to the following interrogatories. Pursuant to FRCP 33, you are required to answer these interrogatories separately and fully in writing, under oath, no later than thirty (30) calendar days after receipt. Responses should be remitted to Joe Smith, Esq., 3200 Main Street, Oldtown, Colorado 80000."

[7] *See* Model Rule of Prof'l Conduct R. 1.6.

[8] Hickman v. Taylor, 329 U.S. 425 (1947).

[9] *See* Fed. R. Evid. 502.

questions and not to obstruct your access to evi-dence.[10] For example, one instruction may direct the party to provide not only information that is in their possession, but information that is reasonably available. Therefore, if the response comes back to you that the party did not have that information in their possession, but you later discover that a co-worker in their department is the person who possesses that sort of information, you can rely on your instructions as part of your argument in a Rule 37 Motion to Compel. (More information about the Motion to Compel can be found in Chapter 8). Generally, instructions should be designed to prompt the opposing party to cooperatively answer the questions you have posed. But if they do not respond to the interrogatories consistent with the instructions, having provided those instructions will strengthen your Rule 37 motion should you need to make it.

Think About This

You have an ethical duty not to lie when answering interrogatories. However, you also have an ethical duty of zealous advocacy to your client that may, even beyond questions of evidentiary privilege, require you not to divulge more information beyond what you are asked. So, when your client is served interrogatories, will you not do everything you ethically can to avoid divulging information? With that in mind, you want to draft your own interrogatories in a manner that limits the other side's opportunities to object or to fail to provide the information you seek.

Definitions

A definitions section should follow your instructions and precede your questions and should be used to limit and tailor the meaning of your questions. Providing definitions may accomplish several things. First, if certain words could be interpreted to have a broad or narrow meaning or if they could actually have several different meanings, the definitions section allows you to instruct the other party as to your intention of how they should be interpreted. Second, it should help you receive the sort of answer you seek. Third, it may limit objections from your opposing counsel.

You don't necessarily have to draft your own definitions from scratch. Many discovery documents are available online and some may have the exact definition you seek. (There is also an example set of interrogatories — including a definitions section — available in the online portion of this text). Some of the better definitions you can simply copy and paste into your definitions section. Other definitions may closely fit your needs but require some editing to fit the facts of your case and your intended meaning. Scrutinize every definition that you use or recycle; assure that it is drafted well to fit the broad or narrow needs of your particular interrogatories.

Finally, you may not find a resource with the definition you need so you will need to independently draft your definition. This is not as hard as it seems; if you know why you need it, and what meaning you intend, your definition should simply reflect those

---

[10] In relevant part, Rule 3.4 provides: "A lawyer shall not: (a) unlawfully obstruct another party's access to evidence . . . [or] (d) in pretrial procedure, make a frivolous discovery request or fail to make reasonably diligent effort to comply with a legally proper discovery request by an opposing party." Model Rule of Prof'l Conduct R 3.4.

intentions. In such a case, consider using a standard or legal dictionary as a starting point or aid.

Form of Interrogatories

The questions can take two general forms: 1) stand-alone questions; or 2) questions with sub-parts. With respect to questions with subparts, each discrete sub-part counts toward your 25-question limit. Because of that limit, it is very important to draft your questions carefully. This requires thought about what you hope to accomplish through the interrogatories, and drafting each interrogatory in a manner that avoids objections or unintended, irrelevant answers.

Most questions can be drafted in stand-alone format. For example, "Identify all company management personnel by name and job title," or, "Identify all documents on which you relied to prepare your answers to these interrogatories." Stand-alone questions should be clear and narrow. In some instances, a question with multiple sub-parts will be better suited for your needs. If you rely on an interrogatory that has an (a), (b), or (c) that follows it, remember that each sub-part may be "discrete" and count toward your 25-question limit. If the sub-parts all relate to the main question they will not have to be counted toward the 25 limit. You will, however, want to consult local rules and case law in your jurisdiction to confirm this, and you will find additional information about what is (and is not) a "sub-part" **LexisNexis Web Course** that comes with this book.

Fact-Finding Interrogatories vs. Contention Interrogatories

Aside from the two formats for interrogatories, there are also two types of information-seeking interrogatories, fact-finding interrogatories and contention interrogatories. Fact-finding interrogatories are straightforward; they seek facts. Contention interrogatories attempt to narrow your understanding of the opposing party's legal theories by inquiring into their legal contentions.

Generally, most of your interrogatories will seek facts. This includes but is not limited to dates, assets, identities of people, documents, records and their locations, and details about specific events. Fact-finding interrogatories are integral to the early stages of discovery. By acquiring details about records, people, or events, your legal theory can gain more weight or you can alter or narrow your legal theory based on the detailed facts. Additionally, these facts and details will impact your future discovery decisions, such as Rule 34 Document Requests or Rule 30 Depositions: you want to know which documents to request or whom you may wish to depose. Here is an example of a simple fact-finding interrogatory served on a plaintiff who brought suit after allegedly sustaining injuries in a car accident in which he was rear-ended:

(1) Had you ever sustained any sort of back injury prior to this accident?

    (a) If so, describe each injury in detail, including the date of each injury, how it was sustained, the extent of the injury, treatment received, any lingering effects, and the identity and contact information of each doctor that treated you.

These questions only seek facts. Furthermore, based upon the responses, your own legal theory and strategy may change.

Contention interrogatories should be used sparingly, but can serve a useful purpose if you need to narrow the opposing party's legal theories. Typically, defendant's counsel will ask a contention interrogatory to narrow the legal theory behind the claims stated in plaintiff's complaint. However, if the defendant filed counterclaims, or included affirmative defenses in the answer, plaintiff's counsel may also find contention interrogatories useful. For example, in the case involving the car accident described above:

- *Do you contend that the driver of the vehicle that struck you was exceeding the speed limit when you were hit?*

Or, if it was also dusk/dark at the time of the accident:

(1) *Do you contend that your vehicle's lights were on at the time you were rear-ended?*

    (a) *Do you contend that your brake lights were in working order the evening of this accident?*

Ultimately, you should consider using a contention interrogatory if there are particular elements of claims, counterclaims, or affirmative defenses that if narrowed would affect your subsequent discovery decisions. But a word of caution: because interrogatories are usually the first discovery tool employed, a contention interrogatory only tends to be effective if you have enough information from the initial pleading(s), the Rule 26(a) disclosures, and the information your client provided. If you do not have enough initial information, this sort of interrogatory will probably be premature; consider waiting to pose this sort of question until you have gathered more information.

Strategy and Goals

With the formulaic nature of interrogatories, there is a temptation to allow their simplicity and inexpensive nature to cause you to draft them carelessly or consider them a throwaway exercise. To avoid this temptation, determine your goals and strategies before drafting your questions to take best advantage of this discovery tool.

Before you even draft a question, you need a list of the goals, and the general information, that you require in order to move forward with your client's case. Review the available resources to help establish these goals. Those resources may include the complaint or answer/counterclaims, Rule 26(a) disclosures, and relevant jury instructions. Once you review these materials, ask yourself what other information you need, why that information will be helpful, whether or how it will influence future discovery requests, and if the opposing party's legal theory is clear based on their complaint or answer/counterclaims. If the theory is not clear, what information do you need to fill in some of the gaps? Depending on the type of case, the questions you may need to address are:

- how many people seem to be involved,
- what is their role/possible involvement,
- what documents you should seek early on,

- whether you are able to get an idea of the scope of the documents involved, and

- what details and facts must you immediately ascertain that could change your legal theory and lay a foundation for the rest of your discovery plan?

Interrogatories will only be beneficial if you know what facts you seek. By setting forth goals for the interrogatories, you will be less likely to omit an important question and you will be more likely to draft refined questions that are limited in scope and gain the information you actually seek. Once you have outlined your goals and identified your strategy, begin drafting your interrogatories. Double check phrasing of each interrogatory to assure that none of them risk being objected to on the basis that it is overbroad, burdensome or oppressive, irrelevant, privileged, equally available to you (through public records), or that might call for a legal opinion. Make sure the interrogatories are structured to elicit factual responses or, for a contention interrogatory, a clear answer. These facts or theories will influence your future discovery requests so be certain you draft the questions in a manner that will make it extremely difficult for the opposing party to object.

EXERCISE:

Prepare the first set of Interrogatories in your case. Also, prepare a brief memo to the file explaining the decisions you made and strategy you implemented in preparing your interrogatories. Include a reflection on the formation of your identity as a professional lawyer, noting how it was influenced by ethical decisions you made in completing this assignment.

ESTIMATED TIME FOR COMPLETING THIS EXERCISE: Three hours.

LEVEL OF DIFFICULTY: Substantial

AS YOU PREPARE THIS ASSIGNMENT, CONSIDER THE FOLLOWING:

- Did you include the caption, title, introduction, instructions, and definitions?
- Did you double check your interrogatories after editing them to assure that all possible words that could be misinterpreted have been defined within the definitions section?
  - Have you counted your interrogatories, including sub-parts?
  - Did you exceed 25?
  - If you did, what question(s) can be deleted (any duplicative or irrelevant questions?) or what question(s) may be broadened (without losing the clarity of the question)?
  - If you did not, make a notation in your file of the remaining number of interrogatories that are at your disposal for future use.
- Review your list of goals for the interrogatories.
  - Have you drafted an interrogatory that will help you achieve each of those goals? Has anything been omitted?
  - Have you included questions that are irrelevant and will not achieve anything useful?
  - If so, delete the question. It is better to save an interrogatory for a good use later on than waste it on a useless question.
- Re-read each interrogatory to scrutinize the language.
  - Ask yourself:
  - What does the question ask for?
  - Is this what I intended to ask for?
  - Is it too broad?

- Is it clear?
- Can it be interpreted in any way other than what I intended?
- If I were opposing counsel, what objections could I raise (overbroad, burdensome, privileged, asking for a legal conclusion, information that is equally available through other sources)? Revise the phrasing to overcome that objection.
- Did you sign your name to the document?
- Did you include a certificate of service?

ONLINE:

The **LexisNexis Web Course** includes an example set of interrogatories, as well as a quiz to review key requirements of Rule 33.

Chapter 4

ANSWERS TO INTERROGATORIES

OVERVIEW

Once you and your client have been served with interrogatories, you have 30 days to send answers and objections back to the opposing party.[11] Interrogatories can be answered in three possible ways: (1) an answer may be provided (depending on the question it may be a yes, a no, or a more detailed response); (2) the question may be objected to on several possible grounds; or (3) the question may be objected to, but a response may also be provided notwithstanding the objection. When answering interrogatories you will work closely with your client. In the case of a corporation, you will work with your client's designated employee or officer. Although the interrogatories were served on that person, you will review the interrogatories before the client sees them. As a result, when the answers are prepared you will have already determined which questions are objectionable, whether your client should respond, and the extent of the response that is required by the question and the rules of ethics. The strategy you employ when answering interrogatories may be more calculated than when you drafted interrogatories simply because you now must shield your client as much as possible (and as ethically appropriate) by scrutinizing the language of each and every interrogatory.

The Rule in relevant part:

FRCP 33. Interrogatories to Parties

　* * *

   (b) *Answers and Objections.*

      (1) Each interrogatory shall be answered separately and fully in writing under oath, unless it is objected to, in which event the objecting party shall state the reasons for objection and shall answer to the extent the interrogatory is not objectionable.

      (2) The answers are to be signed by the person making them, and the objections signed by the attorney making them.

      (3) The party upon whom the interrogatories have been served shall serve a copy of the answers, and objections if any, within 30 days after the service of the interrogatories. A shorter or longer time may be directed

---

[11] Similar to Rule 33(a), Rule 33(b) allows for an expansion of that 30-day deadline if authorized by the court or if agreed upon by both parties, pursuant to Rule 29. Fed. R. Civ. P. 33(b); *see also* Fed. R. Civ. P. 29.

by the court or, in the absence of such an order, agreed to in writing by the parties subject to Rule 29.

(4) All grounds for an objection to an interrogatory shall be stated with specificity. Any ground not stated in a timely objection is waived unless the party's failure to object is excused by the court for good cause shown.

(5) The party submitting the interrogatories may move for an order under Rule 37(a) with respect to any objection to or other failure to answer an interrogatory.

(c) *Scope; Use at Trial.* Interrogatories may relate to any matters which can be inquired into under Rule 26(b)(1), and the answers may be used to the extent permitted by the rules of evidence.

An interrogatory otherwise proper is not necessarily objectionable merely because an answer to the interrogatory involves an opinion or contention that relates to fact or the application of law to fact, but the court may order that such an interrogatory need not be answered until after designated discovery has been completed or until a pre-trial conference or other later time.

(d) *Option to Produce Business Records.* If the answer to an inter rogatory may be determined by examining, auditing, compiling, abstracting, or summarizing a party's business records (includ ing electronically stored information), and if the burden of deriving or ascertaining the answer will be substantially the same for either party, the responding party may answer by:

(1) specifying the records that must be reviewed in sufficient detail to enable the interrogating party to locate and identify them as readily as the responding party could; and,

(2) giving the interrogating party a reasonable opportunity to examine and audit the records and to make copies, compilations, abstracts, or summaries.

Format

Your answers should include six components: a preamble, original interrogatories, answers and/or objections, signature block, and certificate of service. Like the interrogatories, the preamble in the answer document should be brief. When you draft the answers and/ or objections to each interrogatory, precede those responses with the original question. Label your interrogatories and responses accordingly, i.e. Interrogatory (1), Response (1). The original question may be in a standard font. If so the response should be in boldface, italics, indentation, or any combination thereof to make it easy for the reader to identify it as a response. Even in a situation involving antagonistic litigation, do not confuse this layout with "being nice" or "making it easy" for opposing counsel to review your responses. You should use this layout to cover your own back and your client's. Lack of clarity or accidental misnumbering of the responses could be detrimental to your case.

By prefacing each response with the original question you assure that opposing counsel is reading the proper response to the proper question and is not confusing your response with a different one. What if you made a "minor" clerical error and assigned the wrong number to your response? This could create a variety of problems and both waste your time and your client's money in rectifying an otherwise avoidable problem. Second, by re-typing the interrogatory, you assure that your response reflects the question accurately. What if you accidentally misread a crucial word in the interrogatory? Although that is not an error you want to make or are likely to make, you could argue that the response was an error in good faith and you need to amend it. Even better, it might help you to notice the error in time to alter the response so it reflects the correct question. Finally, by using a different typeface and/or indentation, you leave no room for confusion or identification of your response.

Strategy in Answering Interrogatories

General Strategy

Deciding how to respond to each interrogatory involves a substantial amount of strategy. In addition to having your own case strategy, interrogatories may provide you with insight into the opposing party's legal theories or strategy. Therefore, answering interrogatories requires careful thought, scrutiny of the language used in every interrogatory, strategic consideration of how each response could impact your case, and whether any ethical implications will arise as a result of your response.

Ethics

Before you review the interrogatories to determine whether you should object, whether you should answer, or the extent to which you should answer, you must consider the ethical aspects of your answers. Lawyers must bear in mind the professional standards to which they are bound. Inevitably, this brings up the competing interests of client advocacy and the lawyer's duty as an officer of the court.

Attorneys must zealously represent their clients.[12] This involves protecting each client's legal interests and confidentiality.[13] Many times during discovery this commitment to the client will prompt an attorney to object to certain discovery requests and will compel the attorney to severely limit the amount of information disclosed to opposing counsel. However, an attorney also has an ethical obligation to the court and the profession to not engage in or assist deceitful or deceptive pre-trial actions or unwarranted tactic hinder or delay the opposing party's discovery.[14]

---

[12] "A lawyer must also act with interests of a client with zeal in advocacy upon the client's behalf. A lawyer for every advantage that might be realized for a client." Model Rules of Prof'l Co. 09).

[13] See Fed. R. Evid. 502. Work product is also protected material. *Hickman v. Taylor*, supra, note 8.

[14] "A lawyer shall not: (d) in a pretrial procedure, make a frivolous discovery request or fail to make reasonably diligent effort to comply with a legally proper discovery request by an opposing party." Model Rules of Prof'l Conduct R. 3.4(d). Furthermore, "[t]he procedure of the adversary system contemplates that the evidence in a case is to be marshalled competitively by the contending parties. Fair competition in the adversary system is secured by prohibitions against destruction or concealment of evidence, . . . obstructive tactics in discovery procedure, and the like." *Id.*, R. 3.4 cmt. [1].

Generally, an attorney's duty to the client will control and an attorney must keep in mind that the answer to the interrogatory should not exceed the scope of the question. However, there are occasions where an attorney will not want to provide an answer to an interrogatory because of its damaging nature. In such a case, careful examination of the language of the question, the scope of the question, and the implications of an objection must be weighed before responding so as not to violate any ethical obligations.

General Strategy when Answering

Before you begin answering or objecting to the interrogatories, read them all at least once. If any questions immediately appear to be objectionable make a notation. After reading them once through, consider whether the questions provide insight into the other party's possible legal theories. If so make another notation. Once you have gained an initial impression of the interrogatories, go back and scrutinize each one. Ask yourself several questions:

1. What exactly is the question asking?

2. Is there any language that substantially limits the information the other party seeks?

3. Is the question objectionable?

4. Even if it is objectionable, should I object?

    a. What will an objection accomplish?

    b. Would answering despite an objection hurt or help my client?

    c. How may this response/information, notwithstanding an objection, be perceived by opposing counsel? Will it strengthen our position or will it also expose other avenues to pursue, or weaknesses?

    d. Will an objection result in unreasonable future discovery costs for your client when motions to compel are filed. What if you and your client lose the case and attorneys' fees are awarded to the other party? Would your client want to pay for all the extra costs the other attorney racked up because of your evasive discovery tactics?

5. Even if it is not objectionable, will your client's position be damaged in any way if you provide that information?

    a. If it will, is there any basis for an objection that you did not initially find?

    b. If it will and there is no ethical objection, is there any language in the interrogatory that you can interpret (having considered the definitions provided in the interrogatories) to significantly limit or qualify your response?

    c. If you provide that information, object to the question, or significantly limit your response based on your interpreta tion of the language, are there any ethical rules that you risk violating?

6. Is it a contention interrogatory?

    a. If so, what considerations are there in answering?

    b. To what extent should you answer?

    c. How will this answer impact your case?

7. Would it be better to provide documents for the opposing party's review pursuant to FRCP 33(d) if the volume of documents is so large that it would not only be burdensome and time consuming to review for formulating a response?

    a. Could opposing counsel be discouraged from actually reviewing those documents upon realizing the volume of material they would have to review?

    b. If opposing counsel were given the opportunity to review the documents in lieu of being given an answer to the interrogatory, how time consuming and expensive would it be to review those documents for confidential or privileged material prior to making them available for opposing counsel?

When drafting the answers to interrogatories with your client, be diligent about your word choice. Limit your answer; do not provide information that exceeds the scope of the question. Questions that are objectionable may be worth answering if their answers are not harmful to your client. Opposing counsel may be inclined to pursue a dead end legal theory or may not discover stronger theories if the answers you provide, despite the objection, appear to add weight to the dead end theory. Additionally, the answers may not provide opposing counsel with new or helpful information, which would also not advance discovery for them.

Objections

Objections may seem like an attorney's best option when responding to interrogatories because objections can prevent disclosure of any information. While there may be instances in which an objection serves an important purpose, such as protecting privileged or confidential information, some objections may be a poor choice in light of the client's best interests, at least in the long term. Accordingly, there are a number of considerations to account for when deciding whether or not to object.

The phrasing of an interrogatory may automatically raise an objection, as well as the information sought by it. Read every interrogatory carefully to determine whether it is objectionable on the grounds that it is (1) overbroad (too vague); (2) burdensome or oppressive (providing an answer may be too time consuming and lengthy if there is an excessive amount of information that relates to the answer); (3) privileged (attorney-client, marital communication, attorney work product, or general client confidentiality such as trade secrets); (4) equally available (available via public records); (5) calls for a legal opinion (your client is not qualified to or required to provide any legal conclusions); or (6) irrelevant. A relevance objection will likely not hold water when the opposing party files a Rule 37 motion to compel, but if you feel as though you have a strong argument, you could try. Finally, you may object to an interrogatory that you just do not understand (because it is vague or unclear for some other reason), but you would generally be better off to contact your opposing counsel to seek clarification before lodging an objection.

When determining whether one of the above objections apply, read both the interrogatory and the definitions. Ask yourself: what does the question ask? The subject matter alone may be objectionable. Refer to the definitions; when the definition is applied, the interrogatory may become objectionable, i.e. it might call for a legal conclusion, or alternatively, when read together with the definition, it may be placed in a context that removes the objection.

If you determine that an interrogatory is objectionable, there are other questions you must consider before simply responding with that objection. First, is the entirety of the question objectionable? If not, object in part and respond in part; be clear about which sections of the interrogatory your objection and answer apply to. Second, when offering an objection, consider your client's view of the case:

a.   Will an objection harm his position?

b.   What considerations are there to not object?

c.   Can this information be re-sought in the future in a more expensive way?

d.   If so, would it be in your client's financial interest to provide an answer now, (balancing client costs vs. overall strategy to protect as much information as possible)?

e.   Despite the objection, will an answer be beneficial to your client? In other words, can you make the answer give the impression that the opposition's case is weak in this area because you have been forthcoming with the information?

After this examination, it may be clear that an outright objection is the best way to proceed. Or you may find that disclosure will not harm your client even though the question is objectionable. In such a case, object, but then provide the answer without waiving the objection. For example:

Interrogatory No. 7: Identify and describe any written or oral communications between Plaintiff and Defendant between April 2007 and the present date, which Defendant understood to be an offer for Defendant to manufacture 2,000 transmitters for Plaintiff.

Response to Interrogatory No. 7: Objection. This interrogatory calls for a legal conclusion. Subject to and without waiving this objection, Defendant responds that it made an offer when it made its bid for the project on April 22, 2007, as described in the Response to Interrogatory No. 4.

Ultimately, answers to interrogatories involve balancing several considerations. Strategy, ethical obligations, and the ability to rely on objections to prevent or limit disclosure of information must all be weighed before drafting answers. Where there is leeway, the client's position and financial means will usually guide your decisions on how to respond. Depending on your client's perspective and financial resources, you may be serving him best by answering, particularly if he does not have the means to pay for a lengthy, antagonistic discovery process.

EXERCISE:

Prepare a set of Answers to Interrogatories in response to the set of interrogatories that you received from your opposing counsel in your case. Also, prepare a brief memo to the file explaining the decisions you made and strategy you implemented in preparing your answers. Include a reflection on the formation of your identity as a professional attorney as it was influenced by ethical decisions you made in completing this assignment.

ESTIMATED TIME FOR COMPLETING THIS EXERCISE: Three hours.

LEVEL OF DIFFICULTY: Moderate

AS YOU PREPARE THIS ASSIGNMENT, CONSIDER THE FOLLOWING:

- Do you have the caption, title, and preamble included?
- Review the interrogatories and answers that you received from opposing counsel.
    - Do the answers numerically match up with the number of interrogatories?
    - Have the original interrogatories been included in the answers?
    - Were the questions accurately re-typed?
    - Are the answers set off from the interrogatories by italics, boldface, indentation, or any combination of those features?
- Re-read each interrogatory to scrutinize the language.
    - Ask yourself:
    - What did the interrogatory ask?
    - Did I interpret the question consistent with the definitions provided in the interrogatories?
    - Re-read each response, and ask yourself:
    - Did I appropriately limit the response to the specific nature of the question?
    - If an objection was made, was the objection proper?
    - If so, and a response was provided, did the response note that it was not waiving the objection?
    - Was that answer appropriately limited to the scope of the question or the part of the question that was not objectionable?

- Did you sign your name to the document?
- Did you include a certificate of service?

ONLINE:

The **LexisNexis Web Course** includes an example set of answers to interrogatories, as well as a quiz to review key requirements of Rule 33.

Chapter 5

DOCUMENT REQUESTS

OVERVIEW

Among other things, FRCP 34 allows parties to serve requests for production of documents and electronically stored information (ESI). Under the rule, these requests may also extend to inspection of property. Unlike interrogatories — which to a limited degree can "fish" for basic factual information — requests for production of documents and ESI require a substantial degree of specificity. When drafted well, Rule 34 requests can (and should) yield critical information about your case. The term "documents" in Rule 34 is defined broadly, and includes virtually any kind of record, from e-mails, written correspondence and memos, to graphs, drawings, phone records, and bank statements. Like interrogatories, Rule 34 has only one timing requirement; the requests cannot be served until a Rule 26(f) conference has been held. The Rule provides in relevant part:

Rule 34. Producing Documents, Electronically Stored Information, and Tangible Things, or Entering onto Land, for Inspection and Other Purposes

    (a) *In General.* A party may serve on any other party a request within the scope of Rule 26(b):

        (1) to produce and permit the requesting party or its representative to inspect, copy, test, or sample the following items in the responding party's possession, custody, or control:

            (A) any designated documents or electronically stored information — including writings, drawings, graphs, charts, photographs, sound recordings, images, and other data or data compilations — stored in any medium from which information can be obtained either directly or, if necessary, after translation by the responding party into a reasonably usable form; or

            (B) any designated tangible things; or

        (2) to permit entry onto designated land or other property possessed or controlled by the responding party, so that the requesting party may inspect, measure, survey, photograph, test, or sample the property or any designated object or operation on it.

    (b) *Procedure.*

        (1) Contents of the Request. The request:

(A) must describe with reasonable particularity each item or category of items to be inspected;

(B) must specify a reasonable time, place, and manner for the inspection and for performing the related acts; and

(C) may specify the form or forms in which electronically stored information is to be produced.

Components of a Rule 34 Request for Production of Documents

Like FRCP 33 Interrogatories, FRCP 34 Requests for Production of Documents should always include instructions and definitions. Although the rule does not require them, well-drafted requests that include instructions and definitions will help avoid objections by the party upon whom the requests are served. When narrowly drafted requests are combined with instructions and definitions, the likelihood that the proper documents will be produced can be increased and the likelihood that irrelevant or burdensome amounts of documents will be produced is decreased.

Instructions are useful to both limit and direct the manner in which documents are produced. Because your client bears the up-front burden of discovery expenses, the cost of reproducing documents and your time to sort through them should be a constant consideration. This is especially true for those clients of limited means. Through instructions, an attorney can direct the party upon whom the requests were served to refrain from producing duplicative documents and to simply identify the duplicative documents in the responses. Such an instruction can reduce the cost of copying duplicative items, and would reduce the attorney's time spent sorting through and extracting duplicative documents. Additionally, an instruction that documents be produced as they are kept in the normal course of business may give the attorney insight into other issues regarding related documents or business practices. Although producing documents in such a manner is required by FRCP 34, including it in the instruction serves as a professional reminder to opposing counsel, which might be particularly useful for newer attorneys.

Furthermore, like interrogatories, an instruction may direct the party to provide not only documents that are in their possession, but those that are reasonably available to them. That type of instruction is useful when a response states that the party did not have those documents, but you later discover that a co-worker in their department possessed them. You can then rely on your instructions as part of your argument in a Rule 37 Motion to Compel. In sum, instructions should assist you in encouraging the opposing party to cooperatively respond and produce, or in strengthening a Motion to Compel if documents are not produced consistent with the instructions.

In addition to instructions, a definitions section will also help you avoid objections or failure to produce and could add weight to your Rule 37 Motion to Compel (if needed). A definitions section should follow your instructions and precede your list of document requests. Providing definitions may accomplish several things: first, definitions will help you acquire the exact documents or type of documents you seek. Second, definitions may limit objections. Third, if certain words could be interpreted as having several different meanings, the definitions section can help prevent confusion by instructing opposing counsel party precisely how to interpret the terms and produce what you seek.

Definitions play an integral role in your goals and strategies behind the requests since they narrow or broaden or tailor the meaning of your requests. Without definitions, opposing counsel will read your requests in the most limiting or objectionable manner possible to avoid producing documents. Therefore, when drafting your requests, ask yourself *how narrowly* this or that term could be read and draft your definitions to suit the breadth of your intended request. A few examples of terms that could cause problems that definitions could solve are: "any" and "all," "or" and "and," which can be defined to be read in the conjunctive versus the disjunctive and not read in a manner that limits the response; and "documents," which can be defined in the broadest sense possible.[15] Note the need to specify — with great particularity — what you mean by electronically stored information. The following Chapter (Chapter 6) describes in greater detail the growing problems in document discovery that are posed by the explosion of digital information. Please refer to that Chapter when working on the exercise at the end of this Chapter.

Drafting Requests

The phrasing of document requests requires more specificity than drafting interrogatories typically do. Rule 34(b)(1)(A) establishes this requirement: document requests "must describe with reasonable particularity each item or category of items to be inspected."[16] Therefore, opposing counsel has a rule-based objection when requests are too broad or vague. Of course, broad requests will also not help your case because you will find yourself sifting through boxes of irrelevant documents, and you will waste your time and your client's money.

---

[15] For example, the following definition is long but would prevent opposing counsel from applying their own narrow definition in an effort to avoid producing documents: "**Document**," "**documents**," "**internal communication**," "**internal communications**," "**record**," "**records**," "**written communication**," "**written communications**," and "**written correspondence**" means all data, papers, and books, transcriptions, pictures, drawings or diagrams of every nature, whether transcribed by hand or by some mechanical, electronic, photographic or other means, as well as sound reproductions of oral statements or conversations by whatever means made, including written papers or memoranda which summarize oral conversations, whether in your actual or constructive possession or under your control or not, relating to or pertaining to or in any way to the subject matters in connection which it is used and includes originals, all file copies, all other copies, no matter how prepared and all drafts prepared in connection with such writing, whether used or not, including by way of illustration and not by way of limitation, the following: books; records; reports; contracts; agreements; video, audio and other electronic recordings; memoranda (including written memoranda of telephone conversations, other conversations, discussions, agreements, acts and activities); minutes; diaries; calendars; desk pads; scrapbooks; notes; notebooks; correspondence; drafts; bulletins; electronic mail (e-mail); facsimiles; circulars; forms; pamphlets; notice; statements; journals; postcards; letters; telegrams; publications; inter- and intra-office communications; photocopies; micro-film; maps; drawings; diagrams; sketches; analyses; transcripts; electronically stored information (ESI) and any other documents within defendant's possession, custody or control from which information can be obtained or translated, if necessary, by detection devices into reasonably usable form, i.e. typed in English.

[16] Fed. R. Civ. P. 34(b)(1)(A).

Goals & Strategies

Rule 34(b)(1)(A) may cause concern about how to draft document requests with enough particularity to avoid an objection, or to avoid having irrelevant documents (or an unreasonable amount of them) produced. How do you know which documents to request? Even though document requests are usually at an early stage of discovery, an attorney should still have a sufficient amount of disclosed information to determine what documents are needed to move forward. This information comes from the complaint or answer,[17] 26(a) initial disclosures, answers to interrogatories, and information from the client. Interrogatories in particular are helpful because good ones should yield some information about particular documents that apply to (and illuminate) your legal theory, as well as the identity and location of the custodian of those records.[18]

Information, time, and cost are the three most important considerations when drafting document requests. First, you need to know what kind of information is required for your case:

- What type of case is this?
- Under the elements of the applicable law(s), what must be proved or disproved?
- What sort of documents may contain this information?
- What is your legal theory?
- What documents do you need to support that theory?
- What information do you have that leads you to believe those documents exist?
- If you know of specific documents, do you know who has them or where they are? If not, consider ways to uncover that in formation before filing and serving your document requests.
- How can you properly narrow the scope of the request?
- Can applicable definitions be expanded to yield additional types of relevant documents in a way that will not result in a burdensome request?
- What is the relevant timeframe for these requests? Do you have specific dates? If not, how do you intend to discover or limit that timeframe?

Calculated goals and strategies, together with careful drafting, will put you in position to receive the documents that you are certain the other party possesses and that you need. Also, carefully drafted requests that align with your litigation goals

---

[17] For example, if your case involved an automobile accident, there is probably a police report. While that report is not suitable for a Rule 34 request because it is a public record, it is a good place to start. Obtain a copy of the report from the police department. Is the other driver's insurance information and policy number on the report? If so, you now have certain information that will narrow your request when seeking insurance documents through Rule 34.

[18] In particular, if you asked this final question in your interrogatories: "Identify all the documents and records on which you relied to prepare your answers, and the custodian and location of each of those documents," the answer should be a helpful starting point for FRCP 34 document requests.

and strategies should ideally yield only the relevant information you need. A carelessly drafted request without any strategy behind it could result in a massive amount of unanticipated documents that you will have to sift through just to find the relevant documents that you actually need. In short, more is not necessarily better. Accordingly, before you draft your requests, establish your goals and strategy. Balance the goal of acquiring the maximum amount of information with cost and relevance.

EXERCISE:

Prepare a set of Requests for Production of Documents in your case. Be sure to consider the issues surrounding electronic discovery described in Chapter 6 as you do this exercise. Also, prepare a brief memo to the file explaining the decisions you made and strategy you implemented in preparing this discovery document. Include a reflection on the formation of your identity as a professional attorney as it was influenced by ethical decisions you made in completing this assignment.

ESTIMATED TIME FOR COMPLETING THIS EXERCISE: Three hours.

LEVEL OF DIFFICULTY: Substantial

AS YOU PREPARE THIS ASSIGNMENT, CONSIDER THE FOLLOWING:

(1) Did you include the caption, title, and preamble?

    a. Did you include instructions?

    b. Do the instructions direct the party how to interpret the requests, particularly with respect to relevant date ranges and key terms relevant to the litigation?

    c. Do the instructions remind the party that documents are to be produced as they are kept in the normal course of business?

    d. Do the instructions remind the party how many days they have to respond pursuant to Rule 34, a Rule 29 stipulation between the parties, or a court order?

(2) Did you include definitions?

    a. Review your requests alongside the definitions.

    b. Are there any words missing from the definitions section that should be defined so as not to allow opposing counsel to read the request in a limiting or objectionable manner? If so, add those definitions.

(3) Review each definition.

    a. Are they sufficiently narrow, broad, and/or tailored to your needs?

    b. Have you included a definition of electronically stored information that is narrowly tailored to the types of information that you need?

(4) Review your requests

    a. Review your goals and strategies and legal theories along side the requests.

      b. Have you requested all of the documents you believe exist and that are necessary for your goals and strategies?

(5) Scrutinize the phrasing of each request.

      a. Is it too broad?

      b. Is it objectionable?

      c. If you received these requests would you object? Why? How can you alter the request to avoid the objection?

      d. Is the request detailed enough — that is, did you properly identify the documents, their custodian(s), and their location(s)?

      e. Can you and did you properly limit the dates/timeframe of the documents sought, so only the relevant documents are produced?

(6) Did you include a signature block and did you sign your name?

(7) Did you include a Certificate of Service?

ONLINE:

The **LexisNexis Web Course** includes an example set of Requests for Production of Documents, as well as a quiz to review key requirements of Rule 34.

Chapter 6

eDISCOVERY

OVERVIEW

With the massive growth of the internet and the proliferation of digital information in the last decade, electronically stored information has become one of the most troubling, costly, and time-consuming aspects of the discovery process. "The volume of electronically stored information on an average company's IT system is simply staggering. A single gigabyte of data may hold as many as 75,000 pages of Word documents, or over 100,000 e-mail messages. In the accustomed parlance of discovery, that is about 40 'bankers boxes.' "[19] The IT system also includes its servers and network drives, "each of which may have a storage capacity of several hundred gigabytes. Just one server can store one hundred million or more pages — about several dozen truckloads of documents."[20] Not only the volume of the material, but the specificity with which it must be sought is daunting. For example, a string of e-mails: are they one document or several? What if some contain confidential or privilege material and some do not, or the content in one e-mail is mixed?[21] More than any other type of Rule 34 requests, those that seek ESI must be narrowly and specifically tailored. You must know exactly what you seek (or close to it) because otherwise it may never be produced. Indeed, a broad request may yield such an overwhelming volume of material that you find yourself searching for a needle in a haystack and may never be able to find the specific information you need among all the material that is produced. In addition to the vast amount of irrelevant files that a broad or vague request could yield, such a request is likely to be objectionable.

eDiscovery has spawned a number of cases where a requesting party is suspicious about the thoroughness of a production of electronically stored information. Requesting parties believe that the "smoking gun" exists in an electronic file somewhere in corporate computer storage media. Producing parties are quick to label "fishing expedition" any effort to question the bona fides of an electronic production. Generally speaking, the closer to a "fishing expedition" discovery requests are, the less likely they are to be allowed by the judge assigned to the case. Similarly, the closer it is to finding a "smoking gun," the more likely it will be allowed.[22]

---

[19] Aron U. Raskas, Planning and Controlling Costs in Electronic Discovery, D-1, at D-1, The 2d Annual National Institute on E-Discovery: Practical Solutions for Dealing with Electronically Stored Information (ESI) (American Bar Assoc. Center for Continuing Legal Educ. 2008).

[20] Id.

[21] John M. Barkett, E-Discovery: 20 Questions, A-1 at A-2, The 2d Annual National Institute on E-Discovery, supra. See Muro v. Target Corp., 250 F.R.D. 350 (N.D. Ill. 2007).

[22] Id. at A-9. The LexisNexis Webcourse for this text has links to many of these leading cases.

As you begin to draft the document requests described in Chapter 5, remember that eDiscovery requires careful thought. What are you seeking? If it is e-mail exchanges, between whom were they sent? Between what dates? If they are documents relating to the opposing party's insurance policy or bank account, what account or policy number? Specific types of documents? Between what dates? Many ESI requests will be more complex than these examples, but you must break down the relevant material sought into narrow search requests, so as to receive the most relevant results and minimize the risk of receiving cumulative material.

The Problem of eDiscovery

The three biggest problems posed by eDiscovery are volume, complexity, and cost. Volume is a primary root of the problem. As digital records and digital communication have become the norm and communication is now instantaneous, the volume of discoverable material has exponentially increased. For example, it is not uncommon for each custodian to have 50,000 items for review; this is the equivalent of 200 evidence/document boxes. Hand-in-hand with the problem of volume is the complexity of the material. Electronic documents often have extensive electronic data connected to them (known as "metadata" or "data about data"). For example, a printed copy of an Excel spreadsheet may amount to one printed page. However, the metadata and the formulas used to calculated the data on the spreadsheet are all attached to the document in its electronic form.

Because of these developments, the volume and complexity of discoverable information today can lead to unmanageable costs that in many cases may overwhelm the litigation, or indeed outright discourage the filing of the case in the first instance. One way that is increasingly being employed to address the complexity of electronic discovery is by applying the concept of "proportionality," now contained in Rule 26(b)(2)(B)(iii):

> The burden or expense of the proposed discovery outweighs its likely benefit, considering the needs of the case, the amount in controversy, the parties' resources, the importance of the issues at stake in the action, and the importance of the discovery in resolving the issues.

Solutions

The solutions to the eDiscovery problem include staging discovery, internal e-mail management, refereeing by judges when necessary, and client education. Conducting discovery in stages will help to manage costs, although in order to effectively stage discovery it is very helpful to have a reasonable adversary who is willing to cooperate. First, the "waterfront coverage" request that has for years been used in discovery ("Please provide all documents that address, concern or relate to _____") is now completely out of date and almost invariably causes significant problems in the eDiscovery era. Many lawyers believe today that requesting all of the metadata in early stages of discovery is both unwise and unnecessary. Depending on what a lawyer learns first, he or she can then go deeper and request the underlying metadata on particular documents. Only when counsel has reviewed the disclosed documents, and narrowed them to the relevant and highly useful ones, would a request for metadata be appropriate.

Second, the number of custodians from whom information is sought now must be reduced and carefully targeted. An example of what can go wrong is a recent case in which e-mails were sought from 30 custodians. The result was more than $3 million in production costs, and this did not include search expenses. In a large complex case, breaking eDiscovery into stages can help to reduce the cost, volume, and complexity because requests at each stage can be made more specific, relevant, and calculated.

E-mail

Another significant problem in eDiscovery is created by internal e-mail management, particularly within corporations. The volume of e-mails has typically become so huge that broad requests can yield massive document productions. To cut down on the cost of e-mail production and review, specific search terms should be provided with the initial request when possible. For example, "please provide any e-mails or documents that include the following six search terms: Acme, Vail, PVC pipe, Lindsay, Miller, hotel."

Privilege review is another problem related to — but not limited to — e-mail production. Although conducting discovery in stages will help reduce the need for a massive privilege review, the documents and e-mails that are produced will still need to be checked for privileged content. Technology is evolving in this area and it may soon be possible to run digital searches that will find all the material that is privileged and thus obviate the need for a manual review of every document. However, the technology is not yet mature and even when it is ready some human checking may still be required. In the meantime, internal e-mail management and volume control can help reduce this problem.

Managing the Process with Judges and Clients

Judges increasingly need to be better prepared to referee eDiscovery disputes. If the parties cannot agree, judges must be willing to step in and resolve the issues. Often these may relate to proportionality, as when one party has limited means and another appears to have deep pockets. The concern is to prevent eDiscovery from becoming a club with which to beat the opponent, or to discourage litigation where it is necessary.

Finally, client education and better internal management are essential, particularly for corporate clients. In the wake of recent cases, many in-house counsel are concerned about data retention and the risk of facing criminal sanctions if they do not properly manage their company's data. Most are now aware that once litigation is announced or reasonably foreseen, the company has an obligation to retain everything related to the litigation (known as a "litigation hold"). But questions will remain. For example, how much eDiscovery data is actually "related" to the litigation?

The key to a company's preparation for possible future legal actions is understanding the Information Technology infrastructure and what key employees at the company do. When outside counsel is retained, the in-house attorney must be able to explain the company's infrastructure and data management systems. Essentially, the client must understand the problem from the inside out. The company must also be prepared to identify who the relevant custodians may be for any particular sort of information needed in an upcoming litigation. The company also must understand its employees well: who works with whom and how do they manage their data? A company needs to be capable of finding and collecting any data that could be requested during discovery in an efficient and cost-effective manner.

Conclusion

The only effective way to manage eDiscovery is to ask for cooperation from all sides. Attorneys must accept that the most effective way to deal with the volume, complexity, and cost of eDiscovery is to agree with opposing counsel to a staged discovery process. Cooperation and professionalism in this regard will not only result in better managed discovery, but also will help to control costs. Further, judges must be willing to address the problems of eDiscovery by refereeing whatever disputes arise, especially when issues of proportionality are involved. Finally, corporate clients must be educated prior to the commencement of litigation to understand their role in minimizing the problems, and the costs, from within their own company.

EXERCISE:

Negotiate with your opposing counsel an eDiscovery Plan for the remainder of the litigation, with an immediate focus on the Document Requests just filed by each attorney. Draft that agreement in the form of a letter between you and your opposing counsel, which you both sign. Also, prepare a memo to the file reflecting on the negotiation process, and detailing your strategy and concerns going forward. Include a reflection on the formation of your identity as a professional attorney as it was influenced by ethical decisions you made in completing this assignment.

ESTIMATED TIME FOR COMPLETING THIS EXERCISE: One to two hours.

LEVEL OF DIFFICULTY: Moderate

AS YOU PREPARE THIS ASSIGNMENT, CONSIDER THE FOLLOWING:

In preparing for negotiation with opposing counsel, what did you learn about your own client's custodians of electronically stored information (if any)?

In your eDiscovery negotiation with opposing counsel, what did you learn about your opposing party's custodians?

What did you learn about the forms of ESI that your opposing party has?

What did you learn about the volume of ESI that your opposing party has?

Did you negotiate a mutually agreed upon staged document discovery process?

Will that work effectively for both parties, while keeping the cost down?

ONLINE:

In the **LexisNexis Web Course**, you will find an example eDiscovery Negotiated agreement. You will also find links to the key cases in the eDiscovery area, and examples of large-data visualizations and links to information sites about them.

Chapter 7

ANSWERS TO DOCUMENT REQUESTS

OVERVIEW

Responding to FRCP 34 Document Requests requires a substantial amount of attention to detail and advocacy. The responding attorney must pay careful attention to the scope of the documents requested, and only produce the documents that fit within that scope. He or she must also be sure that no privileged information is disclosed and also that objectionable requests are not overlooked. There may be strategic opportunities in answering an otherwise objectionable request, especially if it is so broad or vague that the documents or ESI involved would be so numerous that opposing counsel would never find relevant material, or would waste a lot of time trying to find that information. If requests are drafted poorly it is not the job of the responding party's attorney to improve or correct that request but rather to advocate for his or her own client.

The attorney for the party served with document requests must, of course, respond to the requests in writing. Pursuant to Rule 34, the documents must be produced along with the written responses. The rule allows, however, for a choice between reproducing the documents or simply making them available for inspection. Each written response — when not noting an objection — should identify the document(s) by Bates Stamp number. Note that documents must be produced "as they are kept in the usual course of business."

The rule in relevant part provides:

Rule 34. Producing Documents, Electronically Stored Information, and Tangible Things, or Entering onto Land, for Inspection and Other Purposes

    * * *

  (b) Procedure.

      * * *

      (2) Responses and Objections.

          (A) Time to Respond. The party to whom the request is directed must respond in writing within 30 days after being served. A shorter or longer time may be stipulated to under Rule 29 or be ordered by the court.

          (B) Responding to Each Item. For each item or category, the response must either state that inspection and related activities will be permitted as requested or state an objection to the request, including the reasons.

(C)   Objections. An objection to part of a request must specify the part and permit inspection of the rest.

(D)   Responding to a Request for Production of Electronically Stored Information. The response may state an objection to a requested form for producing electronically stored information. If the responding party objects to a requested form — or if no form was specified in the request — the party must state the form or forms it intends to use.

(E)   Producing the Documents or Electronically Stored Information. Unless otherwise stipulated or ordered by the court, these procedures apply to producing documents or electronically stored information:

   (i)   A party must produce documents as they are kept in the usual course of business or must organize and label them to correspond to the categories in the request;

   (ii) If a request does not specify a form for producing electronically stored information, a party must produce it in a form or forms in which it is ordinarily maintained or in a reasonably usable form or forms; and

   (iii) A party need not produce the same electronically stored information in more than one form.

(c) Nonparties. As provided in Rule 45, a nonparty may be compelled to produce documents and tangible things or to permit an inspection.

Strategy

If you are a lawyer charged with responding to document requests, your first job is to give the requests a preliminary reading and take note of any that appear to be objectionable or that ask for privileged or confidential information.[23] Additionally, you will need to ask yourself if the other party's legal theory is evident based on the types of documents the requests seek. With that preliminary impression in mind, go back and scrutinize each question closely.

Your primary goal is to prevent disclosure of documents that are privileged or beyond the appropriate scope of discovery in the litigation. That goal can be achieved in part at least through the judicious use of objections — providing of course that the objections do not commit an ethical violation. In many cases, entire documents can be

---

[23] Information not protected by attorney-client privilege may nevertheless be protected through an objection based on confidentiality. For example, an objection based on confidentiality would be made in good faith when the information sought is a company trade secret. Many companies, such as chemical or pharmaceutical corporations depend upon trade secrets and expend substantial expense to protect that information from disclosure. A protective order filed with the court might be the best strategy to preemptively protect such trade secret information from discovery in a litigation.

produced.[24] Similarly, if opposing counsel have good reasons, entire documents can be withheld. Finally, there may also be situations in which documents will need to be redacted (with portions deleted) before they are produced. These determinations can only be made after you have scrutinized the language of the request and the accompanying definitions and instructions. Your job is to read each request from your client's perspective. If they are poorly drafted, the opposing counsel may have done you the favor of creating opportunities for legitimate objections.

As you scrutinize each request to prepare responses, ask yourself the following questions:

1. What is the request specifically asking for?

2. Can the request be read very narrowly, in a manner that requires you to produce only a limited set of documents? Consult the instructions and definitions to determine if your interpretation must change.

3. Is the request so broad that you could reasonably bury the opposing party in documents, most of which are irrelevant?

4. If the information is ESI, can you object that production would be too costly and burdensome?[25]

5. Are any of the requested documents privileged or confidential? (If so, object on that basis and make sure those documents are not produced).

6. If a document is privileged only in part, should you object in part and produce the document with the privileged information redacted? Remember that you will need to prepare a privilege log noting the documents for which you are claiming privilege, and the nature of the privilege you are claiming.

7. If documents are not privileged, could those documents still damage your client's position?

8. If so, is there another ethical objection that can be raised?

9. If you cannot ethically object, scrutinize the contents of the document(s) again. Are there any contents of the document that should be redacted on the basis of confidentiality with third parties, etc.?

10. If they are not privileged or damaging, is there any other reason to object?

---

[24] Model R. Prof. Conduct 3.4.

[25] "While essentially all ESI is potentially subject to discovery, producing parties can now endeavor to exclude certain portions of their ESI from the obligations of discovery by designating it as 'Not Reasonably Accessible [NRA] due to undue burden or cost' under Rule 26[b][2][B]. It is important to note that unlike before, this designation must be affirmatively made in order to be valid. . . . If the requesting party disagrees with the NRA claim, the matter goes to the court for resolution under the Proportionality Rule, wherin the court weighs the stated need against the claimed burden, relying on several factors to make the decision. These factors include: the specificity of the request, the availability of the ESI from other sources, the cost of the discovery vs. the amount in dispute, the resources of the parties, and their incentives to control costs, etc." James M. Wright, Estimating the Cost Burden of E-Discovery: A Better Method, D-9, at D-10, The 2d Annual Nat'l Inst. On E-Discovery, *supra*, note 19. For further information on the complexities raised by electronic discovery, consult Chapter 6.

11. Notwithstanding that objection, and if there is no harm, there is no reason to withhold or redact the documents.

Drafting Responses and Producing Documents

The preparation of responses to Rule 34 document requests includes two primary components: the written answers and/or objections and the compilation of documents that you have determined should be produced. The general layout of the responsive document should be similar to Answers to Interrogatories:

1. Introduction;

2. Reservation of objections;

3. Description of document labels (Bates Stamp & sources);

4. Similar to responses to interrogatories:

   a. Include the request made by opposing counsel;

   b. **Bold** and/or indent your answer or objection;

   c. Is a document Bates Stamp number sufficient, or is there additional information that should be included, and/or is there an objection?

5. Signature block

6. Certificate of Service

The preliminary sections of the formal responsive document serve an important function. First, if you believe that some documents may later be uncovered that pertain to the case and could be produced, you may wish to inform opposing counsel that the documents so far produced have been sent in good faith and after reasonable diligence. You may also want, however, to acknowledge that if other documents are found at a later date you will produce them. This will demonstrate your good faith, and may work to your benefit if documents are later found and produced late and opposing counsel files for sanctions for their late production. Second, the reservation of objections alerts opposing counsel that you have not waived but instead reserve the right to object to further requests at a later time in the litigation. Last, the description of the labels on the documents produced provides opposing counsel with a key to understanding the method you used to identify the documents, and the source of the documents. This description therefore allows you to answer the requests by simply providing the applicable document label or Bates Stamp numbers, while submitting the actual documents in another form (such as on a CD).

During the final step, the documents you produce must be labeled and catalogued in the manner they were kept in the ordinary course of business. Check to be sure that the Bates Stamp numbers align with your written answers. In addition you need to double-check the documents you are producing: do they have any hand-written notations you may have made, or are there any confidential post-it notes still attached? Finally, be sure to keep a copy of what you produce to your opposing counsel. If you receive an inquiry about your answers, it is helpful to have a copy of exactly what you produced so you can refer to it later.

EXERCISE:

Prepare a set of Answers to Document Requests in response to the set of document requests that you received from your opposing counsel. In addition, prepare the attachments — the actual documents that you will provide in response to the request — and index them or Bates number them so the answer document will be clear as to which documents are being produced in response to which requests. Finally, prepare a brief memo to the file explaining the decisions you made and strategy you implemented in preparing this discovery document. Include a reflection on the formation of your identity as a professional attorney as it was influenced by ethical decisions you made in completing this assignment.

ESTIMATED TIME FOR COMPLETING THIS EXERCISE: Four hours.

LEVEL OF DIFFICULTY: Moderate

AS YOU PREPARE THIS ASSIGNMENT, CONSIDER THE FOLLOWING:

Have you prepared answers to all of the document requests?

Have you included general objections where appropriate?

If you have objected to any of them, is your objection reasonably based?

If you are asserting privilege as to any particular documents, have you prepared a privilege log?

In your answers, are the specific documents you are producing clearly referenced?

Are the documents attached and numbered in some way so that it is clear which documents are provided in response to which requests?

Has your client signed the responsive document, and have you signed it with respect to objections?

ONLINE:

In the **LexisNexis Web Course**, you will find an example set of Answers to Document Requests, as well as additional supporting information.

Chapter 8

MOTION TO COMPEL PRODUCTION

OVERVIEW

The contentious nature of the discovery process is arguably most evident when an attorney resorts to a Motion to Compel Production under Rule 37. Through the discovery period it is hoped that the parties will have been able to gain useful information through Rule 26(a) initial disclosures, Rule 33 Interrogatories, and Rule 34 Requests for Production or Inspection. However, when the parties are not cooperating sufficiently the use of those rules can break down. It is, unfortunately, not uncommon for a responding party to refuse to answer, refuse to produce, or provide evasive or incomplete responses to discovery requests. In that situation, Rule 37 is the safety net. Once a failure to respond, disclose, or produce has occurred, an attorney may rely on Rule 37 to compel disclosure — provided he or she has first made a good faith effort to confer with the other party about the dispute. The threat of a Rule 37 motion may often provide all the encouragement an uncooperative attorney needs because if the motion is filed and successful the losing party may be required to pay costs or face other more serious sanctions.

Rule 37 – Help!!!

The primary emphasis of a Rule 37 motion is not to sanction but rather to compel the other party to provide the information sought. However, various options are available to the court, usually depending on the seriousness of the discovery failure, and the intransigence of opposing counsel.

Here is a chart indicating the various uses of Rule 37 at different stages of discovery:

Discovery Attempted	Action that may be Taken to Compel
Rule 26(a) initial disclosures were not provided or were not supplemented; or similarly under 26(e)	Move to compel disclosure per 37(a)(3)(A); move to preclude use of that information by the failing party at trial, in a motion, or at a hearing, in addition to seeking expenses or fees, see 37(c)(1)
Rule 30 or 31 depositions – deponent failed to answer a question asked during deposition	Move to compel an answer per 37(a)(3)(B)(i)
Rule 30(b)(6) or 31(a)(4) – corporation or other entity failed to designate a party to be deposed	Move to compel a designation per 37(a)(3)(B)(ii)

Discovery Attempted	Action that may be Taken to Compel
Rule 33 interrogatories – a party failed to answer one of the questions	Move to compel an answer per 37(a)(3)(B)(iii)
Rule 34 – a party failed to produce documents, failed to respond that inspection will be permitted, or failed to allow inspection	Move to compel production or inspection per 37(a)(3)(B)(iv)
Any of the above: but the party either gave an evasive or incomplete disclosure, answer or response	That evasiveness or incompleteness is treated as a "failure" per 37(a)(4); consult the applicable 37(a)(3) rule
Rule 36 – a party failed to admit what was requested	Under 37(c)(2): "if the requesting party later proves a document to be genuine or the matter to be true, the requesting party may move that the party who failed to admit pay the reasonable expenses, including attorneys fees, incurred in making that proof." There are 4 exceptions – see 37(c)(2)(A)-(D)

If the court grants the motion, or if discovery is provided after the motion is filed, the court may (and in some cases must) award reasonable fees and costs that were incurred by the moving party as a result of the conduct in question. If the court grants the motion and the other party fails to act, the moving party may also seek sanctions. Whether to file a motion to compel usually depends on the lawyer's discovery strategy.

Rule 37's Duty to Confer

Regardless of the discovery that an attorney seeks to compel under Rule 37, the moving party must take certain steps before filing the motion. Rule 37 is not a crutch for attorneys to use because the other party does not appear cooperative or simply has not been responsive. Rather, it is a safety net to be used only after other good faith measures have been taken to secure discovery of particular information, when that information was properly sought. Thus, the moving party must make reasonable efforts to resolve the discovery dispute through communication with opposing counsel. Good faith efforts include phone calls, e-mails and formal written correspondence. The goal is cooperation: the purpose of Rule 37 is not to sanction the other party, but to see that information is obtained with as little lost time and wasted effort as possible. Phone calls and e-mails take little time and can produce the desired effect. But it is wise to follow these sorts of contacts with a letter memorializing the status of the dispute. If the negotiations break down, the correspondence may well be attached to the motion and certify the attempts to confer. Furthermore, in most jurisdictions it is generally considered insufficient just to send an e-mail or leave a voice mail, and then file the motion. The attorney must have some evidence of a response from the opposing party (or a lengthy passage of time with no response) before filing the motion.

Rule 37(a)(1) not only requires that the moving party make a good faith effort to confer with the other party prior to filing the motion, but also requires that the moving party certify to the court that this effort has been undertaken. There are three reasons for doing this certification. First, of course, it is required under the Rule. Second, a certification that includes a breakdown of the attempts to confer and the dates of those attempts may persuade the court that its help is actually needed and prompt the court to consider the motion. Third, whether the court awards reasonable costs and fees to the moving party may depend on whether that party appears to have made sufficient good faith efforts prior to filing the motion.

While the moving attorney will not financially benefit from any award of costs and fees, the attorney has a duty to the client to work with diligence and dedication in the client's interests.[26] The fact that an award of costs and fees is predicated upon the attorney's diligence in rendering a good faith effort to resolve the conflict prior to filing the motion indicates that an attorney should address disputes proactively.

Once good faith efforts are made but nevertheless fail, the attorney may then file a Rule 37 motion to compel. There are two courts where this motion may be filed. Typically, the motion is filed in the court where the action is pending.[27] Alternatively, if discovery is sought from a non-party and that individual or entity is located in a different jurisdiction, the motion should be filed in the appropriate court where the discovery is located or where the deposition will be taken.[28]

Strategy – Should I File?

After discovery is sought, failed to be disclosed, and a good faith effort is undertaken, the attorney must next consider whether to actually file the Rule 37 motion. The decision to file may appear obvious. But there may be situations when refraining from such a motion is the best tactic and an attorney needs to weigh several factors when determining whether to file or not: (1) what form of discovery is at issue, (2) how far along general discovery is, (3) how badly the information is needed, (4) how likely it is that the opposing party needs to use this information, (5) the egregiousness of the conduct, (6) the sanctions that are available for failure to comply if the motion is granted, and (7) whether the presiding judge is known for granting motions and imposing sanctions.

What Form of Discovery Is at Issue?

Complete failures to respond present an obvious problem but are fairly rare. Evasive or incomplete, responses are more common and it is wise for the requesting attorney to thoroughly scrutinize them and the original discovery motion — and to do so in good time. It is never a good idea to let such documents sit around for several weeks. The obvious questions are: did a response provide what the discovery request sought? Were some requests objected to, and if so, why? Before rushing to call opposing counsel and express dissatisfaction at the incomplete response, the attorney should review the discovery request that was submitted. Did the request ask for the

---

[26] Model Rules of Prof'l Conduct R. 1.3 (2009).

[27] Fed. R. Civ. P. 37(a)(2).

[28] *Id.*

information with sufficient detail or was it vague? Opposing counsel is not responsible for responding "incompletely" to a poorly drafted discovery request. If the requests were satisfactory, however, and the responses incomplete or evasive, the attorney should call opposing counsel to inquire, explaining what appears to be wrong. The faults could be the result simply of poor drafting or lack of attention to detail rather than a deliberate act.

Depositions (which are addressed in detail in Chapter 10) create a different set of problems that might lead to a motion to compel. There are three general types of problems that arise in relation to depositions that may prompt an invocation of Rule 37. First, a corporation or entity may fail to designate a person or officer as the deponent in response to a 30(b)(6) request. Second, a deponent may not appear for the deposition. Third, during the deposition the deponent may fail to answer questions or may respond evasively or incompletely.

When a corporation or entity fails to designate a deponent in response to a 30(b)(6) request, a motion to compel that designation may be filed. Because this problem occurs prior to the deposition, little cost or expense will be incurred; it is a nuisance and an inconvenience, but it does not compare to the other two problems. If a deposition is scheduled but the deponent fails to show up, this creates a greater financial burden because the court reporter has been hired and the rest of the day's schedule has been blocked out. When filing a motion to compel an appearance, the costs incurred should be provided to the court.

Still worse problems arise if during a deposition the deponent refuses to answer questions, provides evasive or incomplete answers, or acts in a disruptive manner throughout the process. In such cases an order from the court may be sought at that time or after the rest of the deposition has been completed. Rule 37(a)(3)(C) allows the deposing attorney to choose whether to complete the rest of the deposition or to adjourn the deposition entirely. This choice will often depend on whether the deponent has been difficult throughout the entire process or if the answers sought relate only to specific questions or limited topics that could be handled discretely after a ruling from the court. Scheduling, cost and location may often be a driving force behind that decision. Depositions taken out of state may necessitate immediate action whereas with a local deposition, which may only need minimal follow-up questioning, it may be better to complete the deposition and submit the motion afterward.

If discovery is in an early stage and 26(a) disclosures have not been provided or are seriously deficient, the option to file a Motion to Compel under Rule 37 may appear very attractive. But the first question for a lawyer to consider is: how necessary the undisclosed information is for his or her case? The next question is: how necessary is the undisclosed information for the other party's case? If the information sought is not imperative for an attorney's case but he or she has sufficient knowledge to believe the other party's case depends upon certain witnesses, damages, or insurance, the better option may be to forgo a motion to compel. Rule 37(c)(1) prohibits the use of information or witnesses that fall under Rules 26(a) or (e) if they were not disclosed. The party against whom this sanction is raised may argue that the failure to disclose "was substantially justified or is harmless," exempting them from the sanction. It is undoubtedly a gamble, but there are times when waiting to move to compel for the failure to provide the information or witness at trial may be a stronger strategy.

A similar strategy may apply with regard to other forms of discovery. Of course, the purpose of discovery is to ascertain the necessary information to prove the case or mount a strong defense. Accepting insufficient or evasive answers so as to preclude the other party's later use of that information could backfire. An evasive or incomplete answer may indicate a strong but transparent attempt to limit an attorney's access to damaging information. This may frequently signify a need to push further for information or documents. Discovery must uncover the basic information on which the case is founded and then must build upon it, linking testimony to documents and to actions, all of which prove or disprove the elements of the case. For these reasons, Rule 37 may be just the right tool to push the other party to respond completely — or at times may be the perfect tool to leave alone, relying on later objections to the evidence.

Sanctions

Again, while the emphasis in Rule 37 is to secure a court order compelling discovery, there are several sanctions also available, although they are not granted as often as some attorneys would like. The bulk of the sanctions available under Rule 37 fall under subsection (b). The available sanctions under Rule 37(b)(2)(A) provide the courts with a variety of penalties from which to choose:

(i) directing that the matters embraced in the order or other designated facts be taken as established for purposes of the action, as the prevailing party claims;

(ii) prohibiting the disobedient party from supporting or opposing designated claims or defenses, or from introducing designated matters in evidence;

(iii) striking pleadings in whole or in part;

(iv) staying further proceedings until the order is obeyed;

(v) dismissing the action or proceeding in whole or in part;

(vi) rendering a default judgment against the disobedient party; or

(vii) treating as contempt of court the failure to obey any order except an order to submit to a physical or mental examination.

In place of any of the above seven sanctions, or in addition to them, Rule 37(a)(5) states that "the court must" order the party who failed to comply, their attorney, or both of them to pay the reasonable expenses incurred by the moving party as a result of the failure to produce. According to the Rule, the only exception to an award of costs and fees is when the failure was either "substantially justified" or would be unjust, or if the moving party did not make a good faith effort to obtain the discovery.[29]

Courts, it should be noted, have generally been reluctant to award severe sanctions in discovery disputes. Occasionally they have, but typically judges just want the parties to resolve their disputes — and generally assume that both attorneys have contributed to the problem.

---

[29] Fed. R. Civ. P. 37(a)(5)(A).

Drafting the Motion

A Rule 37 Motion to Compel has several components but need not be a long, complex document. The inclusion of specific information and dates is essential. FRCP 37 and the proper subsections should be relied upon in Federal district courts, and the state counterparts to Rule 37 should be relied upon in state courts. Similarly, brief examples of case law relating to the Rule should be incorporated into the motion from the jurisdiction where the motion will be filed. Although the Rule may seem straightforward, citing relevant case law will help the judge to understand how courts in the same jurisdiction have construed and applied the Rule in the past. A judge may be inclined to issue an order compelling the discovery, but may be less willing to impose sanctions against the uncooperative party and/or the attorney advising that party. If local case law supports the use of sanctions, however, clear and succinct use of that law in the motion may prompt the judge to act. Generally, it is best to keep the motion brief although the following information should be clearly included:

1. What exact information was sought, and on what date(s)?

2. Were there court-imposed or rule-imposed deadlines for the response? If so, when were they and how much time has passed?

3. What good faith efforts were undertaken to resolve this problem? Include dates, methods of communication, and responses. Attach exhibits if letters and e-mail correspondence memorialized these communications. Remember, a certification that a good faith effort was undertaken MUST be included.

4. Ask the court for relief, compelling an answer, response, production, or appearance. The court must be aware of the relief you seek in order to grant or deny the motion or to propose an alternate solution or set of sanctions.

5. Outline costs and expenses that have been incurred as a result of this failure, particularly when deposition expenses are involved.

Conclusion

Rule 37 assures that attorneys have recourse when the opposing party or their counsel are obstructing the discovery process. The good faith effort to confer requirement of Rule 37 is clear about the professional responsibility that the moving party must undertake. It is intended to limit the court's involvement in playing the role of a referee. Whether or not to use Rule 37 and file a Motion to Compel is a strategic decision that an attorney must consider carefully. The type of discovery employed, the information sought, and the weight of that information for each party's case are all elements that also demand consideration. Ultimately, Rule 37 is about supporting the discovery of relevant information. Sanctions, while occasionally available for the most egregious disputes, are only a secondary consideration.

EXERCISE:

Develop arguments in support of a Motion to Compel based on the Answers to Interrogatories and Answers to Document Requests that you have received so far in the litigation from your opposing counsel. Describe and explain those arguments in a memo to the file, with specific references to the discovery responses to which they pertain, and be sure to explain the reasons why you are contemplating filing a motion to compel. Then, confer with your opposing counsel to try to resolve the dispute, and describe those efforts, and the result, in the file memo. Include a reflection on the formation of your identity as a professional attorney as it was influenced by ethical decisions you made in completing this assignment.

ESTIMATED TIME FOR COMPLETING THIS EXERCISE: Two hours.

LEVEL OF DIFFICULTY: Substantial

AS YOU PREPARE THIS ASSIGNMENT, CONSIDER THE FOLLOWING:

Have you called and/or e-mailed opposing counsel to explain your concerns?

How often and how recently?

How did they respond?

If the response was unsatisfactory, what was unsatisfactory about it?

Finally, have you sent a formal letter, alleging the failure to respond and informing opposing counsel that you are now considering resorting to Rule 37?

In your motion, have you certified (and supported with documentary evidence) your attempts to confer?

Have you made clear the precise types of information you have requested and which have not been produced?

Have you made clear what specific relief you are asking the court to grant?

Have you cited local case law when requesting sanctions?

ONLINE:

In **LexisNexis Web Course**, you will find and example Motion to Compel, as well as links to Rule 37, and additional supporting information.

Chapter 9

EXPERT WITNESS DISCLOSURE

OVERVIEW

Expert testimony can add weight and credibility to particular aspects of a lawyer's case at trial. Experts can be quite costly, and the choice of whether or not to offer an expert's testimony requires a careful weighing of the options. Things a lawyer needs to consider include: what aspect of the case requires testimonial support that only an expert can provide? Is there a less expensive alternative to an expert for that part of the case? What kind of an expert is needed, and will the expert be deemed acceptable to the court?

Legal Basis for Expert Testimony

Expert testimony is governed by both the Federal Rules of Civil Procedure (FRCP) and the Federal Rules of Evidence (FRE), as well as relevant case law. FRE 702-705 establish the legal bases for admission of an expert's testimony. FRCP 26(a)(2) sets forth requirements for pre-trial disclosure of the expert and the report that the expert will use as the foundation for expert testimony. Finally, existing case law provides limitations on the extent or admissibility of certain types of expert testimony.[30]

Federal Rule of Evidence 702 and 703 provide as follows:

FRE 702 — Testimony by Expert Witnesses

A witness who is qualified as an expert by knowledge, skill, experience, training, or education may testify in the form of an opinion or otherwise if:

(a) the expert's scientific, technical, or other specialized knowledge will help the trier of fact to understand the evidence or to determine a fact in issue;

(b) the testimony is based on sufficient facts or data;

(c) the testimony is the product of reliable principles and methods; and

(d) the expert has reliably applied the principles and methods to the facts of the case.

---

[30] Daubert v. Merrell Dow Pharm., Inc., 509 U.S. 579 (1993) (holding that the judge is the gatekeeper to determine whether scientific expert testimony has a proper fit of relevance and reliability to the issue at hand, setting forth four factors to determine that "fit"); Daubert v. Merrell Dow Pharm., Inc., 43 F.3d 1311 (9th Cir. 1995); Kumho Tire Co. v. Carmichael, 526 U.S. 137 (1999) (extending *Daubert* to all expert testimony, not just scientific testimony).

FRE 703 — Bases of an Expert's Opinion Testimony

An expert may base an opinion on facts or data in the case that the expert has been made aware of or personally observed. If experts in the particular field would reasonably rely on those kinds of facts or data in forming an opinion on the subject, they need not be admissible for the opinion to be admitted. But if the facts or data would otherwise be inadmissible, the proponent of the opinion may disclose them to the jury only if their probative value in helping the jury evaluate the opinion substantially outweighs their prejudicial effect.

The expert disclosure requirements of Rule 26 are as follows:

FRCP 26(a)(2) — Disclosure of Expert Testimony

(A) <u>In General</u>. In addition to the disclosures required by Rule 26(a)(1), a party must disclose to the other parties the identity of any witness it may use at trial to present evidence under Federal Rule of Evidence 702, 703, or 705.

(B) <u>Written Report</u>. Unless otherwise stipulated or ordered by the court, this disclosure must be accompanied by a written report–prepared and signed by the witness–if the witness is one retained or specially employed to provide expert testimony in the case or one whose duties as the party's employee regularly involve giving expert testimony. The report must contain:

    (i) a complete statement of all opinions the witness will express and the basis and reasons for them;

    (ii) the data or other information considered by the witness in forming them;

    (iii) any exhibits that will be used to summarize or support them;

    (iv) the witness's qualifications, including a list of all publications authored in the previous 10 years;

    (v) a list of all other cases in which, during the previous four years, the witness testified as an expert at trial or by deposition; and

    (vi) a statement of the compensation to be paid for the study and testimony in the case.

(C) <u>Time to Disclose Expert Testimony</u>. A party must make these disclosures at the times and in the sequence that the court orders. Absent a stipulation or a court order, the disclosures must be made:

    (i) at least 90 days before the date set for trial or for the case to be ready for trial; or

    (ii) if the evidence is intended solely to contradict or rebut evidence on the same subject matter identified by another party under Rule 26(a)(2)(B), within 30 days after the other party's disclosure.

(D) <u>Supplementing the Disclosure</u>. The parties must supplement these disclosures when required under Rule 26(e).

Determining the Need for an Expert

If you are a lawyer about to pursue a case in which an expert witness may be useful, you need to ask yourself a number of questions. Number one, of course, is whether you even need an expert at all. Expert witnesses can be expensive and your client may not have the financial means to pay for one. Some litigations, however, may demand an expert's testimony to persuade the finder of fact on a particularly technical or scientific aspect of your client's claims or defenses. It is necessary to examine your claims or defenses carefully and consider them in contrast to the strongest arguments that the opposing party will likely present. Then ask yourself these further follow-up questions:

1. What are the areas of your case for which an expert could provide supportive testimony and have you listed them?

2. Why do you need an "expert" for those areas?

3. Is there a less expensive method of convincing a jury of those arguments without losing credibility or persuasiveness?

4. Have you prioritized or clustered all the points on the list in order of those most in need of an expert?

5. Why are the prioritized points important? (Because if some appear to be less important than others, you can consider removing them).

6. Is the nature of any of those remaining experts' reports going to be cost prohibitive — will it outweigh the value of the testimony?

This step-wise process should leave you with only a few possible topics for expert testimony. At this point, pick the expert(s) that you think will have the greatest impact, or have the best credentials to meet your needs. Once you have identified an expert with the qualifications to address your priority areas, ask yourself:

1. What specifically do you want them to address in their testimony?

2. Why is this testimony important?

3. Are there any elements of FRE 702-705 and case law that you need to consider before moving ahead with this expert?

4. Can you now narrow the list further or are you convinced that the expert you have chosen is well suited to the needs of your case and your client's budget?

Preparation of Expert Disclosure

As you select the expert or experts, keep in mind that you must not disclose confidential information to them or you may have waived the privilege not to disclose such information. Also, keep in mind that any drafts of the expert's report are usually discoverable and a sharp attorney will ask for such drafts when deposing the opposing party's expert.

Once you have decided that you will use a particular expert or experts at trial, their identities and reports must be disclosed to the other party. FRCP 26(a)(2)(B) lists six requirements that must be included in an expert's report:

(i)   a complete statement of all opinions the witness will express and the basis and reasons for them;

(ii) the data or other information considered by the witness in forming them;

(iii) any exhibits that will be used to summarize or support them;

(iv) the witness's qualifications, including a list of all publications authored in the previous 10 years;

(v)   a list of all other cases in which, during the previous four years, the witness testified as an expert at trial or by deposition; and

(vi) a statement of the compensation to be paid for the study and testimony in the case.

Although this disclosure may give you the feeling that you are exposing your trial strategy, the disclosure is not optional. Because it is mandatory, opposing counsel must also disclose their expert witnesses. However, these mutual disclosures will not reveal or undermine your strategy if you chose your expert well. Some experts are used to advance an affirmative legal theory while others are used to rebut the other side's expert. If your expert is being used for rebuttal, he may reduce or eliminate any advantage the other side thought they would gain by presenting their expert. On the other hand, if your expert is being presented as a proponent of one of your own arguments, the weight and credibility of his report may help you to convince the jury of the merit of your position. Depending on the strength of each party's experts and expert reports, the "battle of the experts" can be a factor that prompts the parties to enter into settlement negotiations.

EXERCISE:

Prepare an Expert Witness Disclosure in your case. Think through what sort of expert you would like to have to support all or part of your client's theory of the case. Internet based research can help you to find an expert that will fit the bill. Download their CV, and append it to your document disclosing the expert, and describe the nature of the expert's expected testimony. Also, prepare a brief memo to the file explaining the decisions you made and strategy you implemented in preparing the Expert Witness Disclosure. Include a reflection on the formation of your identity as a professional attorney as it was influenced by ethical decisions you made in completing this assignment.

ESTIMATED TIME FOR COMPLETING THIS EXERCISE: One to two hours.

LEVEL OF DIFFICULTY: Moderate

AS YOU PREPARE THIS ASSIGNMENT, CONSIDER THE FOLLOWING:

How and where did you find the expert?

Did you describe the nature of the expert testimony they will offer?

Did you append the CV for the expert?

Have you explained in your memo to the file the strategy you are implementing in selecting this expert, and your plans for how you will use this expert to advance the theory of your client's case?

ONLINE:

In the **LexisNexis Web Course**, you will find links to sites where you can find Expert Witnesses for various types of cases. You will also find an example Expert Witness Disclosure document.

Chapter 10

DEPOSITIONS OF FACT AND EXPERT WITNESSES

OVERVIEW

FRCP 30 provides guidelines and requirements for taking depositions. Leave of court to depose a party or other person is not required, but a party is limited to ten depositions, each of which may not exceed "one day of seven hours." FRCP 30(d)(2). Because of the limits on and cost of conducting depositions, it is important for an attorney to be selective about whom to depose.

Unlike all other forms of discovery, a deposition is live and the witness — even if well coached — may divulge information that would not otherwise have come to light. Indeed, the human factor and live nature of depositions allow the attorney to change the direction and substance of his or her questions in direct response to the deponent's answers. In order to take best advantage of this, a lawyer must go into depositions well aware of what information he or she needs or hopes to acquire and yet mentally prepared to shift attention to unexpected information being offered. It can be a balancing act — paying attention to the expected information, noting each piece of fresh material, and deciding whether that information should be pursued further, and to do all of this even if it deviates from an original strategic plan for the deposition and to be able to do so on the fly. Obviously, given the value of being so nimble in the middle of a deposition, thorough preparation well in advance is essential. As the great coach John Wooden once said of basketball: *"The time to prepare isn't after you have been given the opportunity. It's long before that opportunity arises. Once the opportunity arrives, it's too late to prepare."*[31]

Strategy

Depositions, like all other forms of discovery, will be largely a waste of time and effort unless the lawyer establishes his or her goals and strategies beforehand. An attorney needs to know what information he or she hopes to gain from the deposition and must have planned beforehand how to accomplish that. But the lawyer must also not be bound to this plan, since it is always important to be flexible during a deposition. Deponents often answer questions in unexpected ways. An attorney must be open to their answers and ready to follow them down whatever path they expose since it may lead to other unanticipated information that might help the case.

The need to obtain certain information but also to be flexible necessitates a variety of preparation strategies and materials. Before the lawyer commences drafting an

---

[31] John R. Wooden, Wooden: A Lifetime of Observations and Reflections On and Off the Court 130 (1997).

outline or script, he or she should consider several questions:

(1)　Who do I want to depose?

(2)　Why will that deposition be useful?

(3)　What information do I need to learn from that deponent?

(4)　How do I intend to accomplish this?

When considering the second question, a lawyer should reflect upon the identities of the potential deponents and their relation to the case. Are they the defendant(s) or plaintiff(s); are they employees of a corporate party to the case; or are they a third party who is not directly involved in the lawsuit? Who the deponent is in relation to the case could influence both the tone and phrasing of the questions you ask. If the deponent is a representative of a party to the litigation, any accusatory language might put them on the defensive and cause them to limit the rest of their answers or to be evasive. If the deponent is a third party, a lawyer is wise to keep the language neutral to enhance the deponent's presumed neutrality. In general, as opposed to the adversarial nature of cross examination at trial, depositions present an opportunity for a more relaxed, even conversational, discussion with a witness who could harm your client's case.

Preparation

In addition to being nimble during a deposition and prepared to change directions, a lawyer also needs to be prepared to keep track of the deponent's attitude and emotions. The lawyer must recognize when she or he is losing control of the deponent, when a situation is becoming antagonistic, or when the deponent's emotions get out of hand — all of which could adversely affect or limit the amount and type of information the deponent provides. The lawyer must also think about what methods she or he might use to defuse the situation, to change the tone, and to allow the deponent to compose themselves. A lawyer's own demeanor is important; a deponent will not only respond to the language and tone of a question, but also to facial expressions and body language. A lawyer preparing for a deposition should ask him or herself whether they have a plan to make the deponent feel relaxed, comfortable and conversational. And also to look inwards: Do I have any personal tendencies that could be weaknesses during the deposition such as a short temper, a tendency to respond to antagonism with antagonism, or to respond to answers with facial expressions of disdain, smugness, or annoyance? Obviously, limiting and controlling such tendencies is recommended, since the focus in a deposition should be on the deponent, not the attorney.

Questions

A lawyer planning to take a deposition needs to know or consider a number of other factors as well. For starters there is the vital matter of preparing questions and exhibits, and how best to do it. Preparation of questions can take a number of forms and it could be beneficial to try out all of them, particularly if you are new to taking depositions. Among those forms are: (1) a script of entirely pre-drafted questions; (2) an outline; or (3) if you are more visually oriented, a grid breaking down specific issues or information by topic.

It might be good to draft all three types of deposition preparation documents since the flow of the deposition, the cooperation of the deponent, or the revealing of unexpected information could surprise you during the deposition. At that point you might realize that a script or a topic-based grid or an outline would have been the more beneficial approach. It is better to enter a deposition with a prepared approach you do not end up utilizing than discovering mid-deposition that an alternate document such as an outline would have kept you on track better. The worst thing that could happen would be to deviate entirely from your script, lose track of what issues are imperative and run out of time before you remember to inquire about those issues.

A script should be relatively straightforward. Draft all the questions you intend to ask in the order you wish to ask them. Limit each question to one fact and keep the questions as concise as possible. If you ask a compound question, it might be unclear at trial what the yes or no was referring to or whether it was referring to both parts of the question. In addition, compound questions are often subject to an objection, which might interrupt your flow and control in the deposition. It may be easier to start the script with a topic or issue-oriented outline and fill in the questions based on each issue. Beginning with an outline will create a logical flow to the questions. Additionally, an introductory section may be helpful even if you do not think you will rely on a script for the duration of the deposition. It may help you feel more comfortable and confident at the outset by having pre-written questions and statements.

An introduction accomplishes a number of important preliminary matters, and often includes such elements as:

1. introducing yourself;

2. thanking the deponent for being there;

3. asking them if they have ever been deposed before;

4. explaining the process: why they are there, the purpose of the court reporter, that you will be asking a series of questions, etc.;

5. asking them:

   a. to respond to questions verbally as opposed to head nods (since head movements will not be captured in the transcript);

   b. explaining that you will clarify any question if they do not understand it; and

   c. to feel free to interrupt you if you accidentally cut them off before they are finished answering a question; and

   d. asking them if they understand everything you just explained or asked.

These preliminary statements and questions may help put you at ease but more importantly, they will often put a deponent more at ease (few people have ever been deposed before). Because these preliminary matters all appear on the court reporter's transcript this also assures that a deponent cannot later state in trial that they did not understand the process.

A script may make you feel confident that you have drafted every conceivable question that relates to a topic or to specific information that you need to pursue and assures that you have not omitted anything. However, a script can also throw you off your game because a deposition can take an unexpected turn, delving further into information or areas you did not anticipate. If you feel tied to your script, you may be reluctant to deviate from it and might end up foregoing the opportunity to pursue an unexpected answer that the deponent has provided and could be asked to elaborate upon. Similarly, if you maintain your focus on the script instead of the answers, you may not even realize what beneficial alternate avenues of questioning the deponent may have exposed.

On the other hand, if you get flustered in the middle of the deposition or have deviated so far that you need to loop back to more relevant topics, a script can provide a valuable assist to ease into other topics without having to create questions on the fly. In such situations, the amount of time it takes you to find the next line of questioning in the script from which you can resume the deposition will not be reflected in the printed copy of the deposition. The court reporter does not log the lapse of time in between questions, but merely each question or statement made by the parties to the deposition.

Unlike a script, an outline or grid should only require a glance during a deposition. Its content may be similar to an outline but a grid will break down the outline into a bare-bones topic-based structure. (If you are new to taking depositions, and are not sure which format will help you most, you might prepare both). Because an outline or grid provides key words or phrases, it might be more helpful to keep you on track and aware of the key issues you want to address. The outline's content may vary depending on the type of case and the deponent — and on whether you intend to have a more developed outline as a back-up. If when drafting your script you wrote several questions that you want to ask verbatim, you can always copy and paste those questions directly onto your outline.

An outline or grid can be highly useful since it can keep you on track while still keeping your attention on the deponent. Not being bound to a script, you are more apt to pay full attention to what the deponent is telling you. Your follow-up questions, therefore, will be more responsive to their answers, will keep your thought process focused on where those answers could lead, and will prompt the deposition to be more of a conversation than an inquisition. Once you have exhausted any avenue that the deponent has exposed, all you need is to return to your outline or grid to re-direct the questioning back to a relevant topic that you have not yet pursued. When deposing an opponent's witness, it is common for the tone of the deposition to become adversarial. In such instances, you are almost guaranteed to deviate from a script because you want to pin down the deponent's answers. If the deponent is very uncooperative, a grid or an outline can be very beneficial when you need to get back on track.

Exhibits

The proper preparation of exhibits will prevent you from wasting time sorting through documents during the deposition and will convey your confidence and competence to the deponent and to opposing counsel. A list of documents that are relevant to the deponent should be developed prior to or as you draft your script or outline. Once the first draft of the script or outline is complete, refer back to the list of relevant documents. Review the draft and be sure that you included questions (or key words) that relate to those documents. Assign exhibit numbers to each document in the order that the documents will be addressed. Once the exhibits are numbered, make a notation in your outline and/or script, next to the relevant question or topic so you can remember to produce it and inquire about it during the deposition.

Compilation of the exhibits is a relatively simple and straightforward task but requires attention to detail. You should not only arrange them in the order you believe you will present them, but also review them to be sure that internal notations or privileged and confidential information is redacted or removed before you make copies. Finally, make at least four copies of each: one for you, one for the court reporter, one for the deponent, and one for the deponent's attorney. If other interested individuals will be present, adjust the number of copies accordingly. By providing everyone with a copy, time spent waiting for each party to review the document will be minimized.

Conclusion

As is true with all legal skills, a deposition is only as good as the preparation that went into it. The better prepared you are, the more comfortable you may feel, the more control you may have, and the more likely you are to maximize your time and opportunity with the deponent. Over time you may develop your own method for preparing questions, but until you find that method, take the time to prepare a variety of approaches to questioning, including a script and outline or grid. You will be better served by being over-prepared to make the most of the deposition, rather than being under-prepared. This preparation includes selectively choosing deponents, establishing goals and strategy for each deposition thoroughly preparing a script, outline, and/or grid, and having your exhibits ready to go on the day of the deposition.

EXERCISE:

Prepare an outline for the deposition you have been assigned to conduct in your case. Also, prepare a brief memo to the file explaining the decisions you made and the strategy you plan to implement during the conduct of the deposition. Include your own reflections about the process of preparing to take a deposition. Also include a reflection on the formation of your identity as a professional attorney as it was influenced by ethical decisions you made in preparing for, and conducting, your deposition.

ESTIMATED TIME FOR COMPLETING THIS EXERCISE: Four hours.

LEVEL OF DIFFICULTY: Substantial

AS YOU PREPARE THIS ASSIGNMENT, CONSIDER THE FOLLOWING:

If you are able to actually conduct the deposition and review a transcript, as you review the transcript, consider the following questions:

Did you ask everything you wanted to ask?

Were any of your questions compound questions?

Did the deponent seem to understand all your questions?

Does the transcript indicate that you said "Okay" or "Yes" after many of the answers of deponent?

Did you handle the introduction of documents correctly — by having sufficient number of copies, and by providing a foundation before asking the deponent about the document?

Were there any breaches of ethics or decorum by either party?

ONLINE:

In the **LexisNexis Web Course,** you will find video clips of good and bad depositions of both fact witnesses and expert witnesses. You will also find an example Deposition Outline, as well as a brochure that is often used by practitioners to prepare their own witnesses for a deposition.

Chapter 11

REQUESTS FOR ADMISSION

OVERVIEW

Requests for admission usually (although not always) come near the end of the discovery period since they are designed primarily to narrow issues for trial. Governed by FRCP 36 they are — like interrogatories — an inexpensive discovery tool. Requests for admission are not typically designed to discover any new information. Indeed, in some senses they summarize information that has already been determined in the discovery period. They are designed to establish facts as admitted before trial so those facts do not need to be established at trial.

There are several fundamental aspects of this discovery tool that a lawyer needs to keep in mind when drafting requests for admission. First, as with all forms of discovery, they are limited to the proper scope of discovery as defined in Rule 26(b)(1). Within that scope, allowable requests to admit are limited to those that include established facts, documents and the application of law to certain facts.[32]. Second, unless otherwise ordered by the court, there is no limit to the number of admissions a lawyer may seek, in contrast to the strict limits of interrogatories. Finally, a counselor may serve requests to admit immediately following the Rule 26(f) conference, but only in rare circumstances are they proffered that early in a litigation.

Goals and Strategy

Like all the other discovery tools, requests for admission need goals and a strategy to be most effective. By the time a lawyer is ready to serve Rule 36 requests, he or she will have established a general strategy for the case and it will most likely dictate how he or she will approach requests for admission. If counsel has not yet determined a strategy, the lawyer will need to review all the discovery or pleadings that have been produced and any statements or documents the client has shared, and from those materials figure out what the strongest arguments at trial or in settlement negotiations will be. It is impossible for a lawyer to know what facts and matters need to be resolved by a request for admission until a strategy has been set. For example, if a crucial part of a cross examination at trial will focus on the contents of a document, the lawyer will want to be certain that the document and its entire contents are genuine. If the witness testifies otherwise or contradicts content in the document, the admission of the document's genuineness can be used to impeach the witness.

If you are a lawyer on a case and have refined your legal theory and strategy, you

---

[32] Fed. R. Civ. P. 36(a)(1)

will be ready to address the matters and facts on which your case will partially rest. Start by asking yourself several questions:

1. What facts or application of law to fact do you need to establish?

2. Are these facts all that you need to establish your position?

3. Do you possess any documents that require an admission as to their genuineness?

4. In addition to documents received from the other party during discovery, do you have documents that you acquired from your client or a third party and allegedly belonged to or originated from the party on whom you are serving the requests for admission?

5. How will these admissions (if obtained) influence the rest of a case and any plan you have for settlement negotiations?

6. How can you carefully draft your requests to accurately reflect the knowledge you have and the admission you seek?

7. Do some requests depend on foundational admissions?

8. Keep in mind that you need to include those initial requests. Even if the other party avoids admitting or simply denies certain facts, are there related facts that you can get them to admit to that can help mitigate an issue in settlement negotiations, or lead to a shorter trial?

Drafting

The later requests for admission are served, the more refined and specific the phrasing can be; by the later stages of discovery you will know quite precisely what you need for your legal theory to be strengthened. However, it is possible that under certain circumstances you could serve effective requests in the early stages of discovery.

The most challenging aspect of drafting requests for admission is keeping them simple. Each request should be confined to one narrow fact or matter. Unless the court orders otherwise, there is no limit on the number of requests that can be served, something that you can use to your advantage. For example, if an important document contains facts that you want admitted and if you want the genuineness of the document admitted, break up the requests into a series of short narrow requests.

Review any definitions you may already have used in other discovery documents and incorporate them along with new ones, if necessary. As before, definitions will limit the opportunity of opposing counsel to read the request in an objectionable manner or with an interpretation you did not intend.

EXERCISE:

Prepare a set of Requests to Admit in your case (you may only have a few). Prepare a memo to the file explaining your strategy and thinking as you prepared the Request to Admit document. Include a reflection on the formation of your identity as a professional attorney as it was influenced by ethical decisions you made in completing this assignment.

ESTIMATED TIME FOR COMPLETING THIS EXERCISE: One hour.

LEVEL OF DIFFICULTY: Light

AS YOU PREPARE THIS ASSIGNMENT, CONSIDER THE FOLLOWING:

As you review your requests, determine whether you have separated compound statements into two distinct statements. Re-read each request and ask yourself:

1. Does the phrasing leave room for interpretation or does it clearly state what you intend it to mean?

2. Have you included copies of the documents for which you seek an admission of genuineness and appropriately identified them in the request by Bates Stamp number?

3. Have you made a personal notation in your files about which document goes with which request? (The last thing you want to happen is to receive responses and not know which documents were referenced and which were not.)

ONLINE:

In the **LexisNexis Web Course**, you will find an example set of Requests to Admit, as well as a link to view the full rule, and a quiz regarding key aspects of Rule 36.

Chapter 12

ANSWERS TO REQUESTS FOR ADMISSION

OVERVIEW

As with all other discovery requests, a party receiving requests for admission must respond to them. Every request for admission for which a lawyer prepares responses should, of course, be scrutinized carefully, but because answers to requests for admission involve a client in making *admissions* in the case, they require an even greater level of attention. By answering requests for admission, a lawyer and his client are either outright admitting (or denying) a fact, or a matter, or the genuineness of a document — unless an objection is raised.

Rule 36 provides that, unless otherwise stipulated in writing or ordered by the court, answers must be filed within 30 days from the date any discovery requests were served. This date is particularly important with respect to requests to admit because if answers are not provided within that period, the matters requested by the other party are *deemed admitted*. Failure to timely respond could therefore be devastating to a client and might even earn the attorney a malpractice claim. The Rule also establishes standards with which the answers must comply:

Rule 36. Requests for Admission

(a) Scope and Procedure.

* * *

(4) Answer. If a matter is not admitted, the answer must specifically deny it or state in detail why the answering party cannot truthfully admit or deny it. A denial must fairly respond to the substance of the matter; and when good faith requires that a party qualify an answer or deny only a part of a matter, the answer must specify the part admitted and qualify or deny the rest. The answering party may assert lack of knowledge or information as a reason for failing to admit or deny only if the party states that it has made reasonable inquiry and that the information it knows or can readily obtain is insufficient to enable it to admit or deny.

(5) Objections. The grounds for objecting to a request must be stated. A party must not object solely on the ground that the request presents a genuine issue for trial.

(6) Motion Regarding the Sufficiency of an Answer or Objection. The requesting party may move to determine the sufficiency of an answer or objection. Unless the court finds an objection justified, it must order that an answer be

served. On finding that an answer does not comply with this rule, the court may order either that the matter is admitted or that an amended answer be served. The court may defer its final decision until a pretrial conference or a specified time before trial. Rule 37(a)(5) applies to an award of expenses.

Goals and Strategy

As always, a lawyer's primary goal in formulating responses is to zealously but ethically advocate for his or her client. Therefore, unless there is no way to deny the admission, or making the admission will not damage the case, a lawyer is best advised to avoid admitting anything that can be construed as objectionable or that obviously should be denied. The sanctions described in Rule 36(a)(6), above, are very specific, however, and could be highly damaging to a case so — even more than is normal — a lawyer's objections and denials must be well founded and made in good faith.

The general strategy is simple: scrutinize the language of the requests with great care. Read them. Read them again and read them narrowly unless otherwise compelled by definitions provided in the introductory section. Sometimes even experienced advocates must read a request multiple times before he or she can figure out just how narrowly it can (and perhaps even should) be read. That effort and attention to detail can turn an admission into an admission in part and a denial in part, or can generate a valid objection.

Context is important, too. If a lawyer determines that an admission may work into the opposing party's legal theory it may prompt him or her to view the request differently. Similarly, he needs to examine every word and ask himself:

1. Does the phrasing of the request imply anything beyond what his or her client is willing to admit?

2. Does the pretext of the question raise an objection or a denial or a partial objection?

3. Consider the "why" and "how":

   • Why is this admission important to them?

   • How could an admission influence their legal theory?

   • How could an admission influence one's own legal theory or defenses?

Once a lawyer has scrutinized the requests, he/she should move on to the strategic process of actually answering the request. There are five different ways to respond to a request for admission. First, as we have seen, the request can be admitted. Second, the request can be denied. Third, the request can be admitted in part and denied in part. Fourth, an objection can be raised in place of an admission or denial. Fifth, a lawyer can "neither admit nor deny." This last option is tricky, though, since the reason for any inability to either admit or deny the request must then be explained.

If you are preparing to respond to a request to admit, you will need to employ the following mental regimen:

1. Is your first instinct that the statement is true and therefore should be admitted?

     i. If not, consider a denial — if you are *sure* that it is in fact not true. A mistake might invite a motion for Rule 37 sanctions.

  2. If your first instinct is that it should probably be admitted, ask yourself whether the request is objectionable.

     i. On what grounds can you object?

    ii. Can it be admitted despite the objection? Is there any harm in that? Why or why not?

  3. Is your first instinct that it should be admitted in part and denied in part?

     i. Does either response involve ethical violations? Does a narrow reading of the request bring you into conflict with any ethical rules?

    ii. How much can you limit or qualify your response? Why do you want to do that for this request?

When you have completed these steps in your analysis, you can begin to draft your responses. They should be very clear and as concise as possible. If your response is a simple admission or denial, then that is all that you need to write: "Admit" or "Deny." When you deny something, be certain that you do not need to qualify or explain the denial. Similarly, if you object, make sure that you provide a succinct basis for your objection, particularly in light of Rule 36(a)(6). Finally, if you admit in part and deny in part, make sure you have specified exactly what you are admitting to, what you are denying, and the grounds for the denial. This is an instance in which you want opposing counsel to know exactly where you stand on certain matters. Something that you deny or deny in part may be important to one of the strongest legal theories that your opposing party intends to advance during trial or during settlement negotiations. You do not want to leave confusion about what you have denied or, in some instances, why you have denied something.

Finally, the general format of Rule 36 answers should be the same as those you would use in answers to interrogatories. It is important to include the original statements found in the requests for admission in the body of your responses. When you draft the admissions, denials and/or objections, precede those responses with the original question or statement. Label the requests and responses accordingly, i.e., Request (1), Response (1). If the original statement is in a standard font, the response should stand out in a way to make it easy for the reader to identify it; this can be achieved through using boldface, italics, indentation, or any combination thereof. Particularly with requests for admission, lack of clarity could be detrimental to your client's case.

When you preface each response with the original statement, you assure that opposing counsel is reading the proper response to the proper request for admission and is not confusing your response with a different statement. In addition, by re-typing the statement, you assure that your responses reflect the statement accurately. Finally, by using a different typeface and/or indentation, you leave no room for confusion as to which is your response.

EXERCISE:

Prepare a set of Answers to Requests to Admit in response to the set of Requests to Admit that you received from the opposing counsel in your case. Also, prepare a brief memo to the file explaining the decisions you made and strategy you implemented in preparing the document. Include a reflection on the formation of your identity as a professional attorney as it was influenced by ethical decisions you made in completing this assignment.

ESTIMATED TIME FOR COMPLETING THIS EXERCISE: Two hours.

LEVEL OF DIFFICULTY: Slight

AS YOU PREPARE THIS ASSIGNMENT, CONSIDER THE FOLLOWING:

Have you prepared answers to all of the Requests to Admit?

Have you included general objections where appropriate?

If you have objected to any of them, is your objection reasonably based?

If you have admitted a request in part, and denied a request in part, is it clear which part you are admitting and which part you are denying?

In your answers, are the specific documents you are referring to clearly referenced?

Has your client signed the responsive document, and have you signed it with respect to objections?

ONLINE:

In the **LexisNexis Web Course,** you will find an example set of Answers to Requests to Admit, as well as a link to view the full rule online, and a quiz regarding strategy involved in answering requests to admit.

Chapter 13

MOTION IN LIMINE

OVERVIEW

While there are several types of motions that can be made during the pendency of a litigation, the one that relates most directly to discovery is the Motion to Compel Production, which is addressed in Chapter 8. Other pre-trial motions, such as a Motion to Dismiss or a Motion for Summary Judgment, may rely on information obtained in discovery, but are less directly related to discovery and — particularly for a Motion to Dismiss — may even be made without the benefit of discovery. But there is one type of pre-trial motion that depends more than others on being successful in obtaining relevant information during discovery, and that is the Motion *in Limine*.

Near the end of the discovery process, and often as part of the trial preparation phase, a Motion *in Limine* that is granted by the court can advance your client's interests substantially. These motions ask the court to make an early ruling — prior to trial — on the inadmissibility of certain evidence. These motions are typically made when you believe that any mention of certain evidence may prejudice a jury, so much so that the jury could not overcome an instruction to disregard the evidence. Obviously, when a judge grants a Motion *in Limine* it can influence the nature, length, and substance of the trial. Most importantly, when granted before pre-trial settlement negotiations, a Motion *in Limine* may have a significant impact on the nature and outcome of the negotiations, particularly if the excluded evidence or testimony was an important aspect of the opposing party's case.

The purpose of a Motion *in Limine* is to bar the subject matter of the evidence or to limit the testimony of witnesses. Arguments in support of such a motion must be grounded in the Rules of Evidence. For example, under FRE 407, evidence of a "subsequent remedial measure" is not admissible because such evidence might make a jury believe that the defendant agrees the remedial measure should have been in place before the plaintiff was injured. For example, in a case involving a car being hit by a train at a crossing, when signs and lights were installed at the crossing after the accident, these would be considered subsequent remedial measures and would not be admissible. The Defendant could ask for an early ruling from the court (through a Motion *in Limine*) to make sure that plaintiff did not try to enter it into evidence and possibly prejudice the jury. Another example of a Motion *in Limine* is known as the *Daubert* motion, after the case that established the standard concerning the admissibility of expert testimony.[33] In such a motion, after an attorney has reviewed an expert report received from the opposing party, he or she might believe that the

---

[33] *See supra*, note 30.

expert is not qualified in all the areas that the report addresses. In such a case, a Motion *in Limine* under the *Daubert* standard would be the appropriate vehicle to limit the expert's testimony to only those fields in which he or she is in fact an expert.

When Should You Use a Motion in Limine?

Throughout the discovery process, evidence will be disclosed by a variety of methods including the required initial disclosures and interrogatories, document requests, and depositions, as well as in expert reports. Through each stage in discovery your opponent's strategy and theory of the case will gradually be revealed, but this is particularly true near the end of discovery. In particular, responses to Requests for Admission (addressed in Chapter 12) may begin to reveal specific strategies and plans of the opposing party. In addition, Rule 26(a)(3) requires that the parties file a pre-trial disclosure with the court, which will usually also reveal the strategies and plans for trial of your opposing party. It is at this time that a Motion *in Limine* may be particularly useful.

While the objective of the discovery phase is to obtain all the evidence your opponent may rely upon, you may not have achieved that objective perfectly and — particularly in complex cases — it is rare that you will. Most of the discovery rules were designed to eliminate "surprise" at trial, but in particular, FRCP 26(a)(3) requires that all witnesses, documents, or exhibits must be identified "at least 30 days before trial."[34] The only evidence that either party is permitted to refrain from identifying at that juncture is evidence that will be used solely for impeachment purposes.[35] Because each party is required to make these disclosures it serves to reduce the opportunity for surprise evidence at trial. But it also provides the opportunity to object to the admissibility of evidence intended for use at trial before the trial begins.

Indeed, once you receive the disclosure of evidence that the opposing party intends to present at trial, you must assert any objections you may have to the use of that evidence within 14 days after receiving that information. Although Rule 26(a)(3)(B) states that you are only required to file a list of objections with the grounds for each objection, a decision to file a Motion *in Limine* is generally determined by the complexity of the evidentiary issue. Given the examples provided above, the train/car collision question under FRE 507 is a fairly simple question, and might not even require a Motion *in Limine*, while the *Daubert* motion very likely would.

When a complex Motion *in Limine* has been filed (such as challenging the qualifications of an expert witness your opposing party intends to call) judges will often schedule a pre-trial evidentiary hearing to consider the motion separately. The big advantage to this timing, of course, is that a successful motion — that is, one that excludes evidence the opposing party was planning to rely on — can serve to facilitate settlement.

Clearly, a Motion *in Limine* can be a valuable strategic tool, but whether to use

---

[34] *Id.* 26(a)(3)(B).

[35] *Id.* 26(a)(3)(A).

them will at least partly depend on your overall strategy for any upcoming settlement negotiations. You would not want to file a Motion *in Limine* for the sole purpose of influencing the direction of the settlement negotiations. For one thing, even if it is filed several weeks before negotiations are set to begin there is no guarantee that it will be ruled on prior to that date. If there are a number of motions, the judge may postpone rulings until a comprehensive evidentiary hearing can be held. Or your motion might not be ruled on for weeks because an overwhelming number of motions have piled up on the court's docket, many of which may take priority over your motion. Notwithstanding all this, filing a Motion *in Limine* may still be useful, revealing to your opposing counsel a weakness in his or her case that was not observed during the discovery phase. This may prompt opposing counsel to be more willing to enter into pre-trial settlement negotiations.

Before filing a Motion *in Limine* there are several things to consider: (1) did you refrain from filing a motion to compel certain initial disclosures that you were aware the other party did not disclose; (2) how substantially prejudicial is the evidence involved — that is, does it warrant your time and effort to file a Motion *in Limine* over making an objection during trial; and (3) how many other Motions *in Limine* are you considering and is your client willing to bear the costs involved?

First, as addressed in Chapter 8, when the opposing party fails to make complete initial disclosures, there is a strategic decision whether to file a motion to compel or wait until a later date to request that the court exclude the evidence not disclosed in a timely fashion. Pursuant to Rule 37(c), if the other party fails to make complete (or supplement) their initial disclosures as required by Rule 26(a) and (e), that party may not use that evidence or witness' testimony at trial or at a hearing, unless the omission was harmless or substantially justified.

If you discover a failure to disclose either during discovery or once the complete list of evidence, exhibits, and witnesses is submitted 30 days prior to trial, you must file a motion with the court to exclude the evidence. But be aware that if you knew about this failure to disclose well before you submitted your motion, the court may view the other party's failure to disclose as harmless because you did not take action. The end result could be the court denying your motion. In that situation, your motion must convince the court that your delay in filing the motion was justified and the failure to disclose was not harmless.[36]

You will, of course, want to consider how substantially prejudicial the evidence that you seek to exclude will be at trial. Remember that for evidence to be inadmissible its probative value must be *"substantially* outweighed by the danger of unfair prejudice"[37] or fail to meet other standards under the Federal Rules of Evidence. If the evidence appears substantially prejudicial but could be objected to at trial without any adverse effect on the jury, consider saving the objection for trial against the time and effort it would take to file the motion and supporting brief.

Another consideration is the number and cost of other motions *in limine* you are

---

[36] Model Rules of Prof'l Conduct R. 3.3 (2009).

[37] Fed. R. Evid. 403 (emphasis added).

considering. If you have several grounds upon which to exclude various forms of evidence, but some of those grounds are considerably weaker than others, consider reducing the number of motions you file to the strongest ones. Obviously, drafting these motions takes time and your client may already be challenged by the costs of a trial. On the other hand, if the motion has a good chance of being granted, and it might spur settlement before trial, it might end up saving money by resolving the case sooner.

Conclusion

A Motion *in Limine* can preempt the adverse effects that substantially prejudicial evidence could have on your client at trial. Once you have reviewed the evidence obtained during discovery or through Rule 26(a)(3), you should be able to decide which evidence is of such concern that it might merit a Motion *in Limine*. If successful, it may substantially limit the scope of the trial, and perhaps increase your chances of achieving a favorable settlement prior to trial.

EXERCISE:

Prepare a Motion *in Limine* in your case. Also, prepare a brief memo to the file explaining the decisions you made and strategy you implemented in preparing your motion. Include a reflection on the formation of your identity as a professional attorney as it was influenced by ethical decisions you made in completing this assignment.

ESTIMATED TIME FOR COMPLETING THIS EXERCISE: Three hours.

LEVEL OF DIFFICULTY: Substantial

AS YOU PREPARE THIS ASSIGNMENT, CONSIDER THE FOLLOWING:

Did you explain in your memo to the file why the evidence you seek to exclude would be prejudicial to your client?

Is your argument in the brief grounded in the applicable case law under the Federal Rules of Evidence?

Have you been clear with the judge exactly the sort of evidence you seek to have excluded?

Did you sign your name to the document?

Did you include a certificate of service?

ONLINE:

The **LexisNexis Web Course** includes an example Motion *in Limine*.

Chapter 14

SETTLEMENT

OVERVIEW

No matter how strong a case may seem and how likely a favorable outcome at trial may appear, attorneys should during the course of discovery always have an eye focused towards settlement. Almost 98% of civil cases are resolved before trial through a dispositive motion (i.e. a motion for summary judgment or a motion to dismiss) or by way of a settlement agreement. In addition, various forms of mediation are increasingly being used to facilitate settlement and some jurisdictions promote this type of dispute resolution through court-ordered mediation.

Of course parties are free to enter into settlement negotiations with one another at any point in the pre-trial phase without court involvement. Depending on the relevant facts and legal positions of the parties, and the number of parties involved, the timing of settlement negotiations will vary case-by-case. The most important prerequisite for a settlement negotiation is, of course, meticulous preparation. Every case is about obtaining a favorable outcome for a client. Thorough and strategic preparation for settlement throughout the pre-trial phase is fundamental to delivering your client the best possible outcome.

Preparation and Strategy

Why Settle?

The primary reason for a pre-trial settlement is that trials are expensive and can continue for a protracted period of time, preventing clients from moving on or gaining the monetary damages they seek (and in some cases may desperately need). Settlement negotiations can often result in agreements that limit the attorneys' fees and other costs that would otherwise be spent on trial — and in many cases can result in a better outcome for the client than a trial verdict.

For example, in a personal injury case resulting from a serious automobile accident, the defendant who caused the accident and his insurance company might calculate that a jury award could be as high as $3.5 million — although a far lower award might be possible because of some unfavorable facts in the plaintiff's case. The defendant and the insurance firm are aware that the plaintiff is in dire need of money to pay for medical bills, home remodeling for handicap accessibility and in-home care. Therefore, after calculating the added cost of attorneys' fees and costs of going to trial — and the risk that the award could be on the higher end — the insurance company might decide to, in effect, split the difference. It could conclude that it would be better off to settle for, say, $2.2 million. For his part, the plaintiff might accept this lower offer so as to avoid the risk of a still lower award that might result from a full trial, and so that he can move on and pay for the treatment and care he desperately needs. In this situation, both parties would receive a potentially "better outcome" than a trial might produce, and without the delays and the costs that a trial would have incurred.

Settlement can be reached through a variety of methods, including mediation, settlement conferences with a judge, or settlement negotiations between the parties through their attorneys. Settlement negotiations between the attorneys allow parties the most leeway for two reasons: (1) the attorneys can structure the time, place, duration, and cost of the negotiations more freely; and (2) there are few rules governing or limiting the process because there is no judge or third party mediator involved. As a result, the attorneys control the process, guided by their strategies and their clients' needs and goals.

Why Prepare?

All of the time and effort poured into the discovery process will have been for naught if a lawyer goes into negotiations unprepared and without several strategic plans and creative options in place. Negotiations can be difficult and contentious. In successful negotiations, concessions will be made by both sides to obtain an end result, and if agreed upon, both parties typically will feel as though they are both winners and losers. How much a client "wins" will be considerably influenced by the amount of preparation counsel was able to do in advance. Comprehensively evaluating the facts, legal position, and goals of the client is therefore imperative.

Just as the strengths of each side's legal position regarding both facts and law would have had a significant effect on the likelihood of success at trial, so will they have a significant impact on the terms of a settlement. But the strength of a case is not the only factor — perceptions are also important in settlement negotiations. For example, if a client is in need of money in a quick settlement, her lawyer will want to keep opposing counsel from knowing that since it could put the client at a disadvantage. A lawyer wants the settlement negotiation to be focused not on extraneous concerns but on the facts that have been established in discovery and the law as applied to those facts. The more knowledge the attorney possesses and demonstrates, the more strategic the approach to negotiations can be, and the more able counsel will be to steer the process and formulate an optimal outcome for the client.

How to Prepare?

Preparation for settlement negotiations is a multi-faceted process. Similar to an overall case theory that a lawyer will have developed through the discovery process, a negotiation theory gathers the facts, the applicable law and the evidence. The combination of that information along with the value the two parties place on the case and their varied goals — along with economic and non-economic factors — will influence their willingness to negotiate and will determine the negotiation theory that a competent attorney will employ during negotiations.

(1) Review your litigation chart

If you are a lawyer preparing for settlement negotiations, your starting point should be your litigation plan, which you should have been developing throughout the discovery process (see Chapter 1). A litigation chart will help you assess the strength of your legal position at settlement. Then, you should review the governing statutes and relevant case law, giving particular attention to what elements of proof are required and how much weight is given to each element. Next you will need to turn your attention to the facts, evidence, and expert reports that you have acquired during discovery — what sources of proof do you have for each element and how strong is their support for each element? Also, you will need to evaluate the credibility of each fact, piece of evidence, and its source. Compare this to your perceived impression of the opposing party's case.

(2) Evaluate the likely outcome at trial in relation to jury verdicts

You may be convinced of the legal strength of your case, but at trial a jury will be the ultimate barometer of your case's strength. Even if you believe your case is strong, you may discover that juries in your jurisdiction have a history of not ruling favorably in cases such as yours or of awarding minimal damages. You should consult published jury verdict reports to evaluate this since such reports may play a crucial role in an opposing counsel's perception of your case's strength.

And you should do the same in evaluating opposing counsel's case. Be sure to research and review the verdict reports in your jurisdiction for cases similar to your own. Additionally, review any opinions from the court of appeals upholding or reversing verdicts for cases similar to your own. The verdict reports and cases will enable you to gauge how a jury in your jurisdiction might rule, and the range of damages awards you might expect. Evaluate how these verdicts and cases might support your strategy for negotiating damages, and how they might limit your options.

(3) Assign a value to the case

Having reviewed the verdict reports and cases that were upheld or reversed, and having analyzed your documentary evidence relating to economic and non-economic cost, you must place a value on the case. At the outset of negotiations you will either have to present your initial offer to opposing counsel or respond to their offer with your own. The credibility of your initial offer is important in proving that it is justified and sets a starting point for making incremental concessions during the negotiation process.

The factors that determine the value of the case will vary based upon the nature of the case and the available sources that enable you to assign line-item values. The law of the jurisdiction will also be a factor. If the applicable statute allows costs and fees to be awarded at trial, you will want to determine the costs of trying the case. As best you can, itemize the costs so that if opposing counsel asks for justifications you can provide them in detail. This will help you to maintain credibility and the strength of your bargaining position.

Assess the losses and damages related to your case and document those values with each item. For example, in a breach of contract case involving the sale of goods, determine the value of the goods based on the original contract; look for lost profits from resale; and evaluate whether there is the potential for lost future business with that third-party distributor or retailer. Each of those individual elements must have a value assigned.

Similarly, personal injury cases must have a sum total which can be justified on the basis of medical costs and predicted future losses. List the medical costs to date, the ongoing and anticipated future medical costs; and any lost past and/or future wages. Also include any support costs — home renovations for handicap accessibility, handicap vehicle, or a caregiver. Ascertain whether any vehicle involved was damaged or totaled. Set an opening value on the client's pain and suffering.

Estimates of pain and suffering can be very difficult because they cannot be supported by documentation (like other costs can be). Also, from a human perspective it is hard to place a set value on such intangibles. In such a situation, refer back to the verdict reports and set a value that is within the range that local juries have awarded and that have similar fact patterns to your client's case.

Do not forget to consider the tax consequences of a potential settlement. Damages attributable to physical injuries are not taxable whereas damages attributable to "pain and suffering" are. The lawyer who is aware of these consequences may have a considerable advantage when assigning values.

In addition to setting a total value on your case for an opening offer, you must be aware of the minimum monetary amount that you are willing to accept. If you have a range of values in mind, this will enable you to stay vigilant during negotiations about certain costs and values that have thresholds or limits for negotiation. It will also provide you with the ability to compromise while justifying which values you are willing to adjust. "[S]tudies indicate that certain negotiation positions tend to result in more successful negotiations. Specifically, those negotiators who start with a high, yet reasoned, initial demand and make smaller concessions during the negotiation typically obtain better negotiation results."[38]

(4) Meet with your client to discuss goals, needs, thresholds, and incentives.

Ultimately, the end result of negotiations must reflect your client's wishes. If the terms are not acceptable or appear much less desirable than a likely trial outcome, the client may not agree to the settlement, or end up being unhappy with it. Therefore, you must be acutely aware of the issues and facts that are most important to the client in order to fashion creative approaches to a settlement offer. Moreover, depending on the relationship your client has with the other party or the information you ascertained during discovery, you may want to discuss with your client what incentives, economic and non-economic, may entice the other party to accept a settlement offer when negotiations approach resolution.

A first step is to understand your own client's goals and needs. Having set a

---

[38] R. Lawrence Dessem, Pretrial Litigation 579 (4th ed. 2007).

value for the case, determine the client's bottom line. The client needs to be aware that the high dollar value you have placed on the case for the purpose of the settlement negotiations will not likely be achieved, but rather is the starting point for negotiations. Determine the client's short-term and long-term goals because money may not be the only thing the client values. In a contract dispute, the parties may have a genuine interest in maintaining their business relationship, particularly if they have a long history of working together. In that situation, discussing the economic and non-economic goals and incentives that are important to your client will enable you to formulate a variety of creative approaches to structuring a settlement. For example, in a workplace sexual harassment lawsuit, negotiations might have come to a standstill when the parties are separated by only $3,000; the defendant's counsel insists that they are not willing to go any higher. Now, you might be aware that a genuine letter of apology would be of great importance to your client and that she or he would be willing to forego that last $3,000 in exchange for the letter. By holding out that non-economic factor until the end, the other party may be more willing to accept that term and settle the case.

Additionally, you will need to understand what issues are less important to your client, and which of those the client is willing to concede in order of priority. Should you find yourself at an impasse during negotiations, you would thus be aware of what can be conceded. When the parties have a prior history, your client may be aware of the other party's immediate needs, long-term goals, or issues that have certain incentives. These issues can make a negotiation more effective because the more the offer reflects the other party's needs, the more likely they are to accept the offer. Similarly, if there are multiple parties who have different or competing interests, you must research or learn from your client what issues and interests are important to which parties. Incentives can enable you to design an offer that is creative and appears to favor the other party, while enabling your client to also walk away satisfied with the settlement terms.

For example, if the parties have a history of engaging in regular contracts for the sale of large volumes of high priced goods and they want to resolve the dispute and work together in the future, as defendant's counsel you could propose an agreement in which your client, the seller, would sell his goods to plaintiff at 30 percent lower than market price for the next three years. This might save the plaintiff several hundred thousand dollars. In addition to a low cash settlement, this may put the total value of the settlement well over the amount in dispute. This might please a client more concerned with keeping immediate damages low and less concerned about lost future profits to only one client, especially if his business is not dependent upon that client. By the same token, with some cash in hand and an agreement for future discounted sales in place, plaintiff may consider himself a winner if it means future profits could increase considerably for three years when the goods are resold. Innovative and creative solutions such as this will often help move negotiations along and will enable you to make fewer concessions on what is most important to your client. The more prepared you are to negotiate with both your client's and the other party's goals, objectives, and incentives in mind, the more likely you are to resolve the case with a favorable settlement agreement.

(5)   Timing of Settlement.

The time at which the settlement negotiations are scheduled during discovery can greatly influence the outcome because the strength of your negotiating position and strategy will be largely rooted in the material information you possess. Meaningful settlement discussions may not occur until each party has exchanged information, such as Rule 26(a) initial disclosures and Rule 34 document requests because neither party has enough information to counsel their client that a particular settlement is the appropriate result. Depending on the information and the situation, negotiations could be best scheduled early in the discovery process or considerably later, closer to a possible trial.

(6)   Evaluating all the factors to formulate your strategy.

Once you have reviewed all of the facets of your settlement position, you must look at them as a whole to set your strategy. The strategy should incorporate all the facets that influence your negotiating position and determine how you want to approach the settlement negotiation. How did your litigation chart match up against the elements that the opposing party must prove or disprove? Depending upon the timing of the negotiations, you may be aware of all of the discovery they have received or you may have little idea of the information upon which they are basing their position if only initial disclosures have been made.

Evaluate the strengths and weaknesses of the attorneys. Are you or is your opposing counsel a seasoned litigator or are you (or opposing counsel) a new practitioner? Experience is not necessarily a determinative factor but it can give you an idea of how tough, formidable, or rigid one party could be, and it can help you avoid underestimating your opposing counsel.

Determine the value placed on your case in the context of the goals, concessions, and incentives that are important to both parties. How does time influence your negotiating position — does your client or does the other party need to settle or can they withstand the years it will take to see a trial through? How will this impact your approach to making or asking for concessions?

Finally, how do you personally intend to approach negotiations? In light of all the information you have examined, formulate a strategy that will enable you to control the settlement talks as much as possible. Do you want to present your offer first or do you want to wait to hear the position of the opposing party? Just as with preparing for depositions, be aware of your body language and facial expressions – negotiations can resemble a poker game and you do not want to reveal to opposing counsel how much you like (or dislike) the direction in which negotiations are moving, particularly if you still have many unresolved issues.

Additionally, be mindful of your verbal communication – for both strategic and ethical reasons. Consider what word choices and voice tones you will use to address some of the more contentious issues and present your client's position. And, while the rules of ethics allow "puffing," you cannot "knowingly make a false statement of material fact or law to a third person," which includes opposing counsel.[39] Decide when and how you will raise certain issues, different suggestions for settlement, and certain concessions. How you present these issues can greatly influence the course of the negotiation.

Conclusion

The success of settlement negotiations strongly correlates to the amount of preparation you are able to complete in advance. Some cases are going to be much stronger than others, but success is relative to the strength and weakness of each party, their legal positions, their goals and incentives, and the ability of their attorneys to fashion settlement offers that minimize the damage or gain a more favorable outcome. Preparation is essential to be able to enter negotiations aware of all the factors and how they interrelate.

---

[39] Model Rules of Prof'l Conduct R. 4.1(a) (2009).

EXERCISE:

Meet with your assigned opposing counsel and negotiate a settlement of your case. When you have reached agreement, prepare a settlement agreement document that memorializes your negotiated settlement, including all terms. Also prepare a memo to your file about the settlement process, how it proceeded, what concessions you had to make to reach settlement, and whether you felt those were appropriate concessions. Include a reflection on the formation of your identity as a professional attorney as it was influenced by ethical decisions you made in completing this assignment.

ESTIMATED TIME FOR COMPLETING THIS EXERCISE: One to two hours.

LEVEL OF DIFFICULTY: Moderate

AS YOU PREPARE THIS ASSIGNMENT, CONSIDER THE FOLLOWING:

Does your settlement agreement contain all the terms of your negotiated settlement?

Does it describe the terms in simple and easy to understand language that is not subject to future misinterpretation or disagreement about what was intended?

Does it contain the standard choice of venue and mediation clauses?

Did you both sign the document?

Have you included an Order of Dismissal to be filed with the court, which you both have also signed?

ONLINE:

In the **LexisNexis Web Course,** you will find an example Settlement Agreement to review in preparation of your own.

PROBLEM SET PRODUCT LIABILITY — PRESCRIPTION DRUG

This book includes a problem set that can be used to provide a context for the exercises at the end of each chapter. In this appendix, you will find a brief case summary for the problem, followed by a Complaint and Answer. This should be enough information to get started on the exercise in Chapter 1: The Litigation Plan. The online portion of the book contains many supporting documents for this problem set, including statements of six different witnesses, records of doctor visits, E-mails between key players, and prescribing information. While one could use any similar problem set with this book, the materials provided here (and online) are intended to create a simulated civil litigation within which each student can prepare the exercises at the end of each chapter. In this way, students can learn discovery law through active learning, and do so in the context of how the rules are used in practice.

The YEAR notation system used in the case summary below and in the complaint, answer, and all the discovery documents, follows a pattern that can be adjusted so the same problem may be used year after year. In the notation system used in the documents for this problem set, [YEAR 9] refers to the current year, and [YEAR 1] refers to the year of the earliest event in the case. You may substitute the current year wherever [YEAR 9] appears, and the current year minus 8 years as the year of the earliest event in the case (and use the same system for years in between). You may also choose to keep the [YEAR (X)] nomenclature.

Case Summary

Gale Hartman v. Gillman Sands Klep, Inc.

The Defendant

Gillman Sands Klep, Inc. (GSK) is one of the largest drug producers in the world. The company recently released a new drug, MaxiLife, which it had developed specifically for Type II diabetes patients. The drug created a new way to regulate insulin levels to reduce the production of free testosterone. Free testosterone is responsible for undesirable, and potentially fatal, side effects, including increased blood pressure and heart disease. GSK is incorporated in Delaware, but does business nationwide. Its corporate headquarters are located in Wayne, Pennsylvania, which is where MaxiLife was developed.

In January [YEAR 3], GSK hired Dr. Dana D. Eggleston, one of the country's top biochemists and physicians, to develop MaxiLife. Dr. Eggleston worked closely with Kelly N. Buchanan, the Vice-President of Development for GSK, in developing the drug. The two met frequently and E-mailed each other with updates and concerns during the process. Buchanan was under great pressure from superiors during this time – MaxiLife was going to be a very lucrative product for GSK, and the sooner it hit the market the better.

In June [YEAR 4], Dr. Eggleston, Kelly, and GSK submitted an Investigational New Drug (IND) application to the Food and Drug Administration's (FDA) Center for Drug Evaluation and Research (CDER). The CDER reviewed the application ad, on August 15, [YEAR 4], the FDA determined that, based on the initial trials and information provided in the IND, MaxiLife was safe enough to be tested among a larger, interstate group of human subjects.

On October 1, [YEAR 4], GSK began, under Kelly and Dr. Eggleston's direction, larger clinical trials in partnership with three nationally regarded clinical trial operators, specifically, National Clinical Trial Centers of American, Inc., in Washington D.C.; McCloud Labs in Los Angeles, California; and Medical Consultants, P.C. in Atlanta, Georgia. While physicians and researchers at each of these centers were in charge of the day-to-day operations, all studies were conducted under the guidance of Dr. Eggleston, including those of a young physician on the team, Dr. Pat Flynn. In addition, GSK continued to conduct a small clinical trial on its own. The results of all four studies were submitted to both the CDER committee assigned to review MaxiLife and GSK.

The initial clinical trials concluded on June 1, [YEAR 5]. Dr. Flynn was responsible for reviewing the studies for negative side effects. After reviewing all the reports, Dr. Flynn determined that MaxiLife increased the risk of heart attacks in a certain patient population. Dr. Flynn put these conclusions into a report, which was submitted to Dr. Eggleston.

Dr. Eggleston and Kelly reviewed the report and modified the patient and physician prescribing leaflets accordingly. On December 1, [YEAR 5], Dr. Eggleston, Kelly, and GSK submitted a New Drug Application (NDA), which included full information on manufacturing specifications, stability, and bioavailability data, method of analysis of each of the dosage forms GSK wanted to market, packaging and labeling for both the consumer and physician leaflets, and the results of toxicological studies not already submitted with the IND.

The CDER committee met and reviewed both the IND and the NDA applications. On March 1, [YEAR 6], the FDA approved MaxiLife for pharmaceutical sale and marketing in the United States. The first rollout of MaxiLife occurred on August 1, [YEAR 6].

The Plaintiff

Gale Hartman is a twenty-seven year old snowboarder and Olympic hopeful. Gale lives and trains in Aspen, Colorado, but travels all across the country competing. Gale won national and international competitions over the past two years, and is gearing up to compete in the next winter Olympics.

Five years ago, Gale was diagnosed with high blood pressure. This was particularly concerning because it had the potential to end Gale's snowboarding career. Because of the dangers associated with high blood pressure, physical activity, and altitude, Gale tried three different high blood pressure medications to help with the condition and eventually found one that worked.

Last year, Gale also received a sponsorship deal from Dirton Snowboards, Inc. The sponsorship deal included various forms of support, which made competing easier for Gale. However, around the same time last year, the medication Gale was taking for the high blood pressure problem became less effective, and Gale began to experience side effects associated with high blood pressure that impaired Gale's ability to compete.

Gale made an appointment with local cardiologist Dr. Kris M. Jackson for January 18, [YEAR 7]. Following a physical examination, blood work, and further consultation, Dr. Jackson prescribed MaxiLife to help reduce Gale's high blood pressure. As a condition of prescribing the medication, however, Gale was to check-in with Dr. Jackson on a monthly basis.

Gale started to take the medication on February 1, [YEAR 7]. During that time period, Gale was seriously committed to pursuing the snow-boarding career and did everything possible to improve the body's aerobic capacity and endurance ability.

Then, on June 21, [YEAR 7], shortly after returning from a trip to the Caribbean at Dirton's expense, Gale suffered a massive heart attack that permanently damaged the heart's left ventricle. Dr. Jackson was Gale's attending physician in the hospital and performed a battery of tests to determine the cause.

As a result of the heart attack, Gale is unable to compete in any snowboarding competitions and has lost the sponsorship deal with Dirton Snowboards. Gale believes that GSK failed to properly warn about the potential side effects that accompanied MaxiLife.

IN THE UNITED STATES DISTRICT COURT
FOR THE DISTRICT OF COLORADO

Civil Action No._____
GALE HARTMAN, Individually,

    Plaintiff,

v.   COMPLAINT

GILLMAN SANDS KLEP, Inc., a
Delaware Corporation;
KELLY N. BUCHANAN, Individually;
DR. DANA EGGLESTON, Individually;
and
DR. PAT FLYNN, Individually;

    Defendants.

_____

Plaintiff, Gale Hartman, by and through his attorneys, Craine, Shore & Brown, LLP, alleges the following:

PARTIES

1. Plaintiff, Gale Hartman, is an Aspen, Colorado resident. He is a twenty-seven year old former professional snowboarder. Snowboarding was his only source of income until he suffered a massive heart attack.

2. Defendant, Gillman Sands Klep, Inc. (GSK), is a Delaware corporation and has its corporate headquarters located in Wayne, Pennsylvania. GSK is a pharmaceutical company that develops, produces, markets, and distributes pharmaceutical products including prescription drugs, biologics, and over-the-counter medications. GSK developed, produced, marketed, and distributed the drug MaxiLife. Defendant GSK is directly responsible for all employees hired to work on all phases of MaxiLife development and final product roll-out.

3. Defendant, Kelly N. Buchanan, is an employee of GSK. Buchanan is the Vice President of Development for GSK. She is responsible for the development of all new and improved drugs and biologics that are produced, marketed, and distributed by GSK, including MaxiLife.

4. Defendant, Dr. Dana Eggleston, was employed by GSK during the development of the drug MaxiLife. Dr. Eggleston was the Head Research Scientist for GSK, on the MaxiLife project. Dr. Eggleston was directly responsible for the scientific development of the drug, for gaining the drug's approval by the FDA, and for overseeing the employees assigned to the scientific facet of the drug's development.

5. Defendant, Dr. Pat Flynn, was employed by GSK during the development of the drug MaxiLife. Dr. Flynn was part of the scientific research team charged with developing MaxiLife and ultimately gaining the drug's approval by the FDA.

JURISDICTION AND VENUE

6. This is a civil action seeking declaratory and injunctive relief against Defendants. This cause of action is based on Defendants' distribution and marketing of the drug MaxiLife without proper warning of its risks. Defendants' failure to properly warn the public of the risks associated with ingestion of the drug harmed Plaintiff by causing him to suffer a massive heart attack, which would not have occurred if Plaintiff's doctor and Plaintiff had been informed of the drug's risks.

7. This court has jurisdiction pursuant to 28 U.S.C. § 1332 because the amount in controversy exceeds $75,000.00 and because Plaintiff and Defendants are residents of different States; Plaintiff resides in Aspen, Colorado and Defendants reside in Pennsylvania and Delaware. Defendants Buchanan, Eggleston, and Flynn reside in Pennsylvania; GSK is a Delaware resident as it is incorporated in Delaware and is a Pennsylvania resident as its corporate headquarters and primary operations occur at the Pennsylvania facility.

8. Venue is proper in this Court pursuant to 28 U.S.C. §§ 1391(a) because a substantial part of the events or omissions giving rise to the claim occurred in Colorado.

BACKGROUND

9. Gale Hartman lives in Aspen, Colorado, and was a professional snowboarder until June [Year 7]. Mr. Hartman competed nationally and internationally and was considered an Olympic hopeful for the [Year 9] Winter Olympics.

10. As a professional snowboarder, Gale Hartman was sponsored by Dirton Snowboards, Inc. ("Dirton"). Winnings from competitions and the salary provided by Dirton were Mr. Hartman's sole source of income in [Year 7].

11. In [Year 1], Mr. Hartman was diagnosed with high blood pressure but otherwise, was in good health. He tried several medications and finally found one that worked, which was LowPress, produced and distributed by Defendant GSK.

12. In [Year 5], LowPress began to lose its effectiveness in treating Mr. Hartman's high blood pressure. Plaintiff began to seek new medication that would effectively treat his condition.

13. In late [Year 6] and early [Year 7], Mr. Hartman saw television advertisements promoting a new GSK drug MaxiLife. He also read the MaxiLife leaflets that were publicly available on GSK's website. Although it was not the primary purpose for the drug, the advertisements indicated that the drug helped treat high blood pressure.

14. In late [Year 6], a GSK pharmaceutical representative directly marketed MaxiLife to Dr. Kris Jackson, a cardiologist in Aspen, Colorado.

15. In January [Year 7], Mr. Hartman met with Dr. Jackson to discuss the non-effectiveness of LowPress in treating his high blood pressure and the possibility of a prescription for MaxiLife. Dr. Jackson conducted further research on the use of MaxiLife to treat high blood pressure by reviewing materials published and distributed by GSK. After additional follow-up with Mr. Hartman, Dr. Jackson prescribed MaxiLife to treat Mr. Hartman's high blood pressure.

16. Mr. Hartman began taking MaxiLife on February 1, [Year 7]. On June 21, [Year 7], he suffered a massive heart attack. As a result of the heart attack, Mr. Hartman has permanent heart damage that renders him completely unable to compete as a snowboarder.

17. As a result of this physical bar to competition, Mr. Hartman lost his sponsorship with Dirton. Without the ability to win competition prize money and without his sponsorship, Mr. Hartman has lost all his sources of income. As a result of the heart attack and continued medical treatment, Plaintiff has mounting medical bills that he cannot afford to pay.

18. Serious health risks are associated with the drug MaxiLife and Defendants did not disclose those risks to the general public through MaxiLife's labels, inserts, marketing materials, and television advertisements. As the result of this failure to disclose these risks, Mr. Hartman was prescribed MaxiLife and ingestion of the drug caused him to suffer a massive heart attack, which permanently damaged his heart and caused him to lose his livelihood.

CAUSE OF ACTION

19. Defendants proximately caused Mr. Hartman's heart attack by failing to warn the public, including Mr. Hartman and his Cardiologist, of the health risks associated with taking the drug MaxiLife. But for this negligent failure to warn of the dangers of the drug, Mr. Hartman and his Cardiologist would not have considered prescribing Mr. Hartman with the drug MaxiLife as they would have known that MaxiLife was not appropriate for patients with high blood pressure.

20. Defendants proximately caused Mr. Hartman to lose his sponsorship with Dirton Snowboards, his ability to professionally compete as a snowboarder, which was his livelihood, and his opportunity to be named to the [Year 9] United States Olympic Snowboarding Team, as a result of his massive heart attack. But for Defendants' negligent actions in failing to warn the public of the dangers and risks associated with the drug MaxiLife, Mr. Hartman would still be an able-bodied professional snowboarder and would not have lost his sponsorship agreement, and sources of income.

WHEREFORE, Plaintiff respectfully requests the following relief:

A. An injunction requiring GSK to immediately issue warnings and an explanation of all the risks associated with ingesting MaxiLife to all doctors with whom GSK has marketed MaxiLife and to all pharmacies that distribute MaxiLife; and to immediately change its television advertisements, marketing materials, website information, its prescribing information, and its package inserts for MaxiLife, highlighting and warning the public of all the risks associated with ingesting MaxiLife.

B.   Damages of $225,000 in lost wages, $500,000 in compensatory damages, and $1,000,000 in punitive damages.

C.   Any other relief as this Court deems just and proper.

Dated: December 14, [Year 7]   Respectfully submitted,

                                                    /s/_____
                                                    Denard P. Craine, Esq.
                                                    Attorney for Plaintiff
                                                    1700 Lincoln Street
                                                    Denver, Colorado 80202

CERTIFICATE OF SERVICE

I hereby certify that a true and correct copy of the foregoing Summons and Complaint was personally served at 11:00AM this 14th day of December, [Year 7], via Process Server, to the attorney of record for Gillman Sands Klep, Inc., a party in this action at the address listed below, and that a true and correct copy of the foregoing Summons and Complaint was personally served at 11:20AM this 14th day of December, [Year 7], via Process Server, to the individual Defendants Dr. Pat Flynn and Kelly N. Buchanan, at the GSK corporate headquarters, 3456 Research Way, Wayne, PA 19087. I hereby certify that a true and correct copy of the foregoing Summons and Complaint was personally served at 1:30PM this 14th day of December, [Year 7], via Process Server, to Dr. Dana Eggleston, a party in this action, at his home address in Media, Pennsylvania:

                                                    /s/_____
                                                    Denard P. Craine
                                                    Attorney for Plaintiff

IN THE UNITED STATES DISTRICT COURT
FOR THE DISTRICT OF COLORADO

Civil Action No._____
GALE HARTMAN, Individually,

Plaintiff,

v.   ANSWER

GILLMAN SANDS KLEP, Inc., a
Delaware Corporation;
KELLY N. BUCHANAN, Individually;
DR. DANA EGGLESTON,
Individually; and
DR. PAT FLYNN, Individually;

Defendants.

Defendants Gilman Sands Klep, Inc. (GSK), Kelly Buchanan, Dr. Dana Buchanan, and Dr. Pat Flynn, by and through their attorneys, Shanahan, McCoy & Powers, LLP, in answer to the Complaint in the above captioned case, admits, denies, and alleges the following:

1. Admits the allegations in paragraphs 1, 2, 3, 4, 5, 7, 8, 9, 10, 14

2. Admits in part and denies in part paragraph 11. Defendants admit that LowPress is manufactured by GSK. Defendants have insufficient information to admit or deny whether Plaintiff was in otherwise good health and whether Plaintiff tried other medications.

3. Defendants have insufficient information to admit or deny the allegations in paragraphs 12, 15, 16, and 17 on the grounds that Defendant's are unaware of Plaintiff's medical history and therefore deny paragraphs 12, 15, 16, and 17.

4. Denies the allegations in paragraphs 6, 13, 18, 19, and 20.

COUNTERCLAIMS

5. Defendants allege that if Plaintiff did not suffer from Type-II diabetes, that Plaintiff did not take the drug for its intended use.

6. Defendants allege that if Plaintiff took MaxiLife for some "off-brand" purpose, that Plaintiff was negligent in his actions.

7. Defendants allege that if Plaintiff did negligently take the drug that he was at fault for any adverse health effects that could possibly be attributed to taking the drug for an unintended purpose.

8. Defendants allege that in the event that if Plaintiff negligently took the drug for an unintended purpose that Plaintiff proximately caused his own illnesses,

adverse health effects, and/or proximate results of those illnesses or adverse health effects.

WHEREFORE, Defendants respectfully request that Plaintiff's request for relief be denied.

Dated: January 8, [Year 8].   Respectfully submitted,

/s/_____
Maria Shanahan, Esq.
Shanahan, McCoy & Powers, LLP
Attorney for Defendants
100 S. Broad Street
Philadelphia, Pennsylvania 19109

CERTIFICATE OF SERVICE

I hereby certify that a true and correct copy of the foregoing Answer was personally served at 10:00AM this 8th day of January [Year 8], via Process Server, to the attorney of record, Denard P. Craine, for Plaintiff, at 1700 Lincoln Street, Denver, Colorado 80202:

/s/_____
Maria Shanahan
Attorney for Defendants